TEN KEY PRINCIPLES OF CHRISTIAN LIVING

ROBERT GRIFFITH

GRACE AND TRUTH PUBLISHING
PO Box 338, Gunnedah NSW 2380 Australia
www.graceandtruthpublishing.com.au

ISBN 978-1-7635504-0-7

TABLE OF CONTENTS

1. HE'S GOD AND WE'RE NOT

Thank you for joining me in this journey where we will be exploring together what I believe to be ten key principles of Christian living. Each chapter will examine a foundational statement or truth about living as a believer today and then unpack that through the Bible and apply it to our lives.

I am sure I could find many more important principles which will apply to our walk with God in Christ, but I have chosen what I believe to be the top ten from my experience as a pastor, teacher and disciple of Jesus. I can assure you that all of these ten principles will begin and end with God. That should be no surprise because the Bible is all about God, and as the Westminster Shorter Catechism reminds us, *"The chief end of man is to glorify God and enjoy Him forever."*

We were made by God and for God. We were made to know God, to serve God, to love God, and to live forever in the presence of God. At some point, every human being must cry out to God with Saint Augustine and say, *"Our hearts are restless until they find rest in You."* We were made to glorify God, and in the act of bringing glory to God, we will enjoy Him forever. In enjoying God, we will then enjoy (in the truest and deepest sense) the life He has given us.

So, what is the first and most basic principle of Christian living? It all starts with one fundamental truth:

He's God and we're not.

Nothing is more basic than that, but I have lost count of the number of times in my spiritual life when I've really needed reminding of this key principle because it's so easy to slip into a mindset which negates this foundational truth.

All spiritual reality begins with this truth, and if we skip, ignore or downplay this first principle, nothing else we encounter in this book will make any sense. In order to help us grasp this foundational principle, I want us to look at a some Bible passages. This key principle is so fundamental that I could easily find a hundred passages to support it, but I'll share just a few here.

Job 23:13 *"But He stands alone, and who can oppose Him? He does whatever He pleases."*

Job understands that he cannot demand anything from the Lord. In and of himself, Job is powerless to change his awful condition and he can't even demand a hearing to plead his case with the Lord. God does what God wants, and Job is powerless to oppose Him. Job understands and accepts this basic reality.

Job 42:2 *"I know that You can do all things; no plan of Yours can be thwarted."*

This verse introduces us to the final chapter of Job's saga. It comes after God has given him a theology lesson and a final examination on creation, which Job then flunked miserably. Thoroughly humbled, Job now confesses that his God is all-powerful, He does what He wants, and no one stands against Him. This confession leads him to deep repentance for his foolish questioning of God's plan.

Psalm 135:6 *"The LORD does whatever pleases him, in the heavens and on the earth, in the seas and all their depths."*

The psalmist goes on to list various proofs that God does what He wants and then the conclusion of the psalm is a five-fold call for everyone to praise the Lord (vv. 19-21).

Daniel 2:20-22 *"Praise be to the name of God for ever and ever; wisdom and power are His. He changes times and seasons; he sets up kings and deposes them. He gives wisdom to the wise and knowledge to the discerning. He reveals deep and hidden things; He knows what lies in darkness, and light dwells with Him."*

When King Nebuchadnezzar of Babylon had a dream, he could not remember it and did not understand, so he asked Daniel to help him. Daniel agreed, prayed to God, and the dream and its interpretation were revealed to him. The above words are part of Daniel's response of praise to God. I am struck by the phrase, *"He knows what lies in darkness."*

God sees even the hidden things because the darkness is not darkness to God. Let's now run the story forward to Daniel chapter 4. When King Nebuchadnezzar takes credit for the greatness of his kingdom, God struck him with a kind of insanity that made him think he was a beast of the field.

For seven years he lived among the wild animals. When he finally turned his heart to the Lord, his sanity was restored. This is part of his public confession to God:

Daniel 4:34-35, 37 *"Then I praised the Most High; I honored and glorified Him who lives forever. His dominion is an eternal dominion; His kingdom endures from generation to generation. All the peoples of the earth are regarded as nothing. He does as He pleases with the powers of heaven and the peoples of the earth.*

No one can hold back His hand or say to Him: 'What have you done?' Now I, Nebuchadnezzar, praise and exalt and glorify the King of heaven, because everything He does is right and all His ways are just. And those who walk in pride He is able to humble."

Here is a pagan king who re-discovered the truth of God's sovereignty the hard way. To his credit, he does not hesitate to speak that truth once his sanity is restored. God does whatever He wants. Even the greatest human rulers are as nothing to God. No one can ever question what God does. Everything God does is right, and the Lord knows how to humble the proud. It would be hard to find a clearer statement of this first principle in the entire Bible.

> **Romans 11:33-36** *"Oh, the depth of the riches of the wisdom and knowledge of God! How unsearchable His judgments, and His paths beyond tracing out! 'Who has known the mind of the Lord? Or who has been His counselor?' 'Who has ever given to God, that God should repay him?' For from Him and through Him and to Him are all things. To Him be the glory forever! Amen."*

This wonderful doxology comes at the end of Paul's presentation of the gospel as God's answer to man's sin, and his presentation of God's future plans for His people. No one could have foreseen how God would respond to human rebellion. No one gives God advice. No one can trace His path across the starry skies. God is never in debt to anyone for any reason. Everything is from Him, everything is through Him, and everything is to Him. And He alone gets the glory.

One of the sections of the Westminster Confession of Faith says that God ordains *"whatsoever comes to pass."* So that means that everything in the universe is either caused by God or allowed by God. Nothing ever 'just happens' and nothing is caused by anyone or anything which is outside God's control. Some things He directly causes; other things He allows to happen; but all things in heaven and on the earth and even the things that happen in hell, even the very acts of Satan, are controlled by God.

Revelation 19:6-7 *"Then I heard what sounded like a great multitude, like the roar of rushing waters and like loud peals of thunder, shouting: 'Hallelujah! For our Lord God Almighty reigns. Let us rejoice and be glad and give Him glory!'"*

When Christ returns to the earth, the whole world will clearly know what we know right now by faith: **Our God reigns.** He reigns over all things. He reigns in every situation. He reigns in the very best circumstances of life and in the very worst. He reigns over His friends and even over His enemies.

He reigns in heaven, and He also reigns in hell. He reigns over those who doubt Him and those who deny Him. He reigns over those who follow other gods and other religions. Our God reigns. The world does not yet see it, and at times even we have trouble believing it because we don't always see it clearly. But the truth remains and will not be changed: Our God reigns.

As I step back and consider all these marvelous verses, one fact jumps out at me and will not be ignored. Every time the Bible writers speak of God's sovereignty, it always leads them to praise.

He does what He pleases ... *praise the Lord.*
No one can oppose Him ... *shout for joy to the Lord.*
Everything God does is right ... *Hallelujah.*
How unsearchable is His wisdom ... *to God be the glory.*
His plan is working out perfectly ... *praise be to God.*
Our God reigns ... *let the people rejoice and be glad.*

If this truth does not fill our hearts with praise, then we either don't understand what the Bible says, or we simply refuse to believe it.

This truth remains whether we believe it or not: God is in charge of all things. Even when it looks like God is not ruling, He's ruling! When chaos appears, He's in charge of the chaos. When things start falling apart, He's even in charge of the falling apart. Theologians call this doctrine the *'The Sovereignty of God.'* You find it on almost every page of the Bible. The word 'sovereign' means king or ruler. God's sovereignty means that He is always calling the shots in the universe. He is in charge of all things.

> **Psalm 24:1** *"The earth is the Lord's, and everything in it, the world, and all who live in it."*

That's what I mean by the statement: *"He's God and we're not."* God is the Creator, and we are His creatures. This is truly the most fundamental principle of spiritual life. Until you understand this, and submit yourself to it, nothing in life will work. So many of our struggles in our Christian journey come from forgetting who's God and who's not.

At this point I want to mention God's freedom. Although we talk a great deal about freedom, it's usually our personal freedom in view. We rarely think about God's freedom, yet that is the major point of the Bible passages above. The bottom line is this: God's freedom is the only <u>true</u> freedom in the entire universe. Every other 'freedom' is a derivative from His freedom in one way or another. Here are seven statements that explain what I mean by God's freedom:

1. God is absolutely free to do whatever He wants to do.

Because God is God, He can do whatever He wants to do, whenever He wants to do it. If He wants to create a planet, or a galaxy, or even another universe, He just says the word and it happens. He is truly 'free' in the absolute sense of the term.

This is why He announced Himself to Moses as "I AM WHO I AM" (Exodus 3:14). God is eternal, self-existent, and entirely self-sufficient. He exists entirely apart from the universe He created.

2. God has the right to deal with us any way He chooses.

By this I mean that God was under no obligation to create you or me or anyone else. He is also under no obligation to keep any of us alive for even one more second. He is under no compulsion to save a single member of the human race. No one has a claim on God. He can do what He wants with any of us, and no one can ever second-guess Him.

3. God doesn't have to treat me the way He treats somebody else.

Many people struggle with this concept because they think that because God did something for a friend or a neighbour or a loved one, then God must be bound to do the same thing for them, but it just doesn't work that way. God may deliver you from cancer and your best friend may die of cancer. Envying your neighbour because he has something you don't have, is a waste of energy because God always treats us as individuals, not as groups.

The truth is, God might do for you exactly what He's done for someone else. He might do more, or He might do less. He might do something entirely different. He is God. He can deal with us the way He chooses.

4. God doesn't have to treat me today the way He treated me yesterday.

This needs to be understood clearly. Since God's character never changes, we know that He is the same yesterday, today and forever. He is always gracious, always loving, always holy, and always just.

His ways are always perfect. However, that doesn't mean that what happened to me yesterday is some kind of pattern or guarantee for what will happen tomorrow.

God's character and His love for me will never change. How His grace and faithfulness and love is expressed, may vary widely from one moment to the next. One day I may enjoy a remarkable answer to prayer. The next day I may be in the valley of suffering, waiting on the Lord to deliver me. He's always the same God but He does not display Himself in my life the same way all the time.

5. God can answer my prayers any way He chooses.

Everyone who has prayed, should understand this truth. One night we fish and catch nothing. The next night our nets are filled to breaking point. I may be in prison one night and an angel may come to set me free, or God may send an earthquake to deliver me. Or I may die in prison as many Christians have over the years. A loved one with a dreaded disease may be spared by God for several years, only to die from that disease eventually.

One day I may sense God's Spirit working so powerfully in my life, another day I may struggle, wondering if God is even listening! So, it goes for all of God's children. Our God is infinitely creative in the way He deals with us as He brings us to spiritual maturity. There are bright days and dark nights, and the Lord is in the middle of both.

6. God will not tolerate any rivals to His throne.

This is one of the clearest themes of the Bible. There is only one God and He demands our exclusive worship. After reminding the Jews that He had delivered them from Egypt, God made this the First Commandment: *"You shall have no other gods before me"* (Exodus 20:3).

That's clear, isn't it? No other gods, period. God is number One and there is no number two. He will not share His glory with another - and that includes us!

7. God is not obligated to live up to my expectations or explain Himself to me.

This may be the most important statement regarding God's freedom. He doesn't bind Himself to do what we expect Him to do. We see in the Bible how God was continually surprising His people. Everything happened just as God promised, but very little worked out exactly the way people expected. He's the God of great surprises and He doesn't have to explain Himself to us.

There are many questions we would all like to ask. Almost always our questions revolve around suffering, sadness, the death of loved ones, and times of personal disappointment.

I have found that the greater the sadness, the less likely we are to fully understand it. Small things we can figure out on our own, but great losses are usually hidden in the mind and heart of God.

> **Deuteronomy 29:29** *"The secret things belong to the Lord our God."*

God is far bigger than we imagine; His presence fills the universe; He is more powerful than we know; wiser than all the wisdom of the wisest men and women; His love is beyond human understanding; His grace has no limits; His holiness is infinite; His ways are past finding out; He is the one true God; He has no beginning and no end; He created all things and all things exist by His divine power; He has no peers; and no one gives Him advice; no one can fully understand Him; He is absolutely perfect in all His ways.

There is nothing we can do, not even our worship and praise, which can add to Who God is. He did not create us because of any lack in Himself. God was not lonely. Were every person on earth to become an atheist, it would not impact who God is in any way. The belief or disbelief of the human race cannot change the reality of who God is.

To believe in Him adds nothing to His perfection; to doubt Him takes nothing away. He rules all things, everywhere, at all times. Nothing escapes His notice. Nothing is beyond His control. He is beyond time and space, yet He controls space and time. Time is actually the brush with which God paints His story on the canvas of human history. Eternity is the perspective from which we view that painting. This is our God!

As we ponder God, we are eventually led to a humbling truth, one that is not mentioned often and is hardly believed when it is taught: **God does not need us.** If any concept flies in the face of contemporary Christianity, this is it. Down deep inside, most of us want to feel that we are important and necessary, and we like to think that God must have needed us, or else why would He have created us? In the absolute sense, God doesn't *need* anything or anyone. He didn't create us because He was in need, and He didn't save us because heaven was empty. He does not need our worship, our gifts, our obedience, our service, our prayers, or anything else from us. There is absolutely no lack of any kind with God.

This is a very humbling, and for many people, also a very frustrating truth. But ask yourself: Do you really think God cannot get along without you? What if your congregation just disappeared today? What if they had never existed? Do you really think that the universe depends on us for its survival? Hardly.

The Pharisees told Jesus to rebuke His cheering disciples as He entered Jerusalem for the final time, He replied, *"If they keep quiet, the stones themselves will cry out"* (Luke 19:40). If He wants to, God can cause the trees to clap their hands and the mountains to sing out His praises. He can even make the rocks cry out in worship! The fact that God created us at all - is an act of His sovereign will. The fact that God saved us – is a miracle of His sovereign grace. The fact that God accepts our worship and rewards our obedience – is a another miracle of His sovereign love.

How then shall we live, in light of this confronting reality? As we ponder the truth of God's freedom, there are many applications which come to mind. Properly understood, it ought to lead us to a calm confidence in God even in the midst of unspeakable tragedy. It should also make us bold in our witness and strong in our prayers. If we believe these truths, we will find the strength to persevere over the long haul, knowing that even our foolish mistakes cannot cancel or thwart God's plans.

The truth of God's freedom ought to lead us to praise and worship. If it doesn't, then we haven't fully understood the biblical teaching. It is not that we will praise God directly for the pain and sadness around us or for the sinful acts of others. But we will praise God that He is able to work in, with, and through everything that happens, both the good and the bad, to accomplish His will, to make us more like Christ, and to bring glory to Himself.

We will say with the psalmist, *"Come, let us bow down in worship, let us kneel before the LORD our Maker!"* (Psalm 95:6).

There is coming a day when *"every knee shall bow, and every tongue confess that Jesus Christ is Lord to the glory of God the Father."* (Philippians 2:9-11).

If that day is coming, then why not get a head start and bow your knee now and confess that God is God and Jesus Christ is your Lord?

The Lord is God and there is no other.

Can you say those words above out loud? Make it a public affirmation of your faith … and here's the good news. If you really mean it, then you can take a deep breath, let God be God and all will be well.

There is abundant joy for those who truly accept the most fundamental truth in the entire universe:

He's God and we're not.

2. GOD DOESN'T NEED US

In the previous chapter, we explored the first principle which teaches us an absolutely fundamental truth: *He's God and we're not.* All spiritual reality must begin at that point. Until we have settled the issue of who's God and who's not, we are still in spiritual kindergarten and if we are fighting against God's right to be God, our lives will be miserable, and we will be forever frustrated. But when we finally come to the point where we can allow God His rightful place in the universe, in His church and in our lives, then we're ready to move on.

That brings us to the second key principle of Christian living, which I touched on in the previous chapter, but I want to elaborate more now. This truth flows from the first and it's the simple fact that, *God Doesn't Need Us.* Of course, we desperately need God, but He doesn't need us.

This principle tells us something about God and something about us. To say that God doesn't need us, means that He is totally and truly sovereign over the universe. He's the boss, the ruler, and the Lord of all things. That means He alone has <u>true</u> freedom, which we touched on in the first chapter.

Go to any Bible college or seminary and you will hear very learned (and sometimes heated) debates about 'free will.' But when we use that term, we almost always refer to human free will. Such debates have always fascinated me – especially when the term 'free will' appears nowhere in the Bible. Here's the truth of the matter. Only one person in the universe has complete free will. Find that person and you've found God. Our 'free will' is drastically limited, God's free will has no limit. He can do whatever He wants to do whenever He wants to do it.

That is the essence of true free will. It's true that we humans have important moral choices to make and it's also true that we are accountable for those choices. But any 'free will' we have is only a derivative. The 'freedom' we have to obey (or to rebel) is a freedom that God has gifted to us.

This second principle also tells us something about God's transcendence, which the Bible teaches when it tells us that, *'God is high and lifted up.'* Transcendence means that God created the universe and is separate from it. The universe is not an extension of God or a necessary part of God. He existed in and of Himself long before the universe was created.

This principle also points us to God's holiness. This is a hard attribute to define because it is basic to who God is. As one writer put it, holiness is what makes God truly God. It's the 'goodness' of God that separates Him from His creation. It involves purity and separation from sin, but goes beyond that. If God were not holy, He would not be God at all.

This principle also impresses upon us the truth of God's immensity. All power and all wisdom and all majesty reside in Him alone. He inhabits all things, and His presence fills every part of the universe. There is nowhere you can go where God is not already there. Not only does this principle tell us something about God, it also tells us something about who we are. To say that we desperately need God, reveals our inherent weakness. We are sinners by birth, by nature and by choice. The true condition of the human race is revealed in these penetrating words from Paul:

> **Romans 3:10-12** *"There is no one righteous, not even one; there is no one who understands, no one who seeks God. All have turned away, they have together become worthless; there is no one who does good, not even one."*

Even a casual reader is struck with the universal, repeated emphasis of these words: *"no one ... not even one ... no one ... no one ... all ... no one ... not even one."* Paul leaves absolutely no room for misunderstanding here! The whole human race has rebelled against God. As a result, when God looks upon humanity He can't find a single righteous person. Not even one. He can't even find anyone who truly seeks Him.

Sin has so warped the human heart that no one does anything truly good in God's sight. We are all 'worthless' in His sight. That last part is a pretty tough pill to swallow. How can you reconcile the word 'worthless' with the truth that *"God so loved the world?"* Why would anyone love that which is worthless? The answer goes to the very heart of this second principle and to the very heart of the gospel of God's amazing grace.

God loves us in spite of our sin and not because of some supposed worth He found in us. To put it in crass terms, He found nothing worth saving in us, but He saved us anyway because that's the kind of God He is. That thought is both humbling and thrilling. None of us deserved God's grace. If we deserved it, it wouldn't be grace. Any 'worth' we have to God is worth that He gives to us. We have value because God values us, not because of anything of value within us.

This second principle exposes our phony independence, our casual arrogance, our sinful pride, and our obsessive need to be in control. It tells us that we aren't in control, and we weren't ever in control, not even when we thought we were. We can find this concept in numerous places in the Bible. Here are just a few:

> **John 15:5** *"I am the vine; you are the branches. If a man remains in me and I in him, he will bear much fruit; apart from me you can do nothing."*

Romans 7:24 *"What a wretched man I am! Who will rescue me from this body of death?"*

1 Corinthians 8:2 *"The man who thinks he knows something does not yet know as he ought to know."*

2 Corinthians 3:4-5 *"Such confidence as this is ours through Christ before God. Not that we are competent in ourselves to claim anything for ourselves, but our competence comes from God."*

As I grow older and wiser, I find myself increasingly glad that we worship a God Whose power is unlimited' Who never grows weary,' 'Whose plans will not be defeated' and 'Whose ways are far beyond my own.'

What a comfort to serve such a God. I need a God like that, and I need Him more than I will ever know. We desperately need God. Sometimes we feel that need, often we don't. But feelings don't matter in any case. The fact is: we desperately need God. So let me just recap:

> God is free to do whatever He wants to do whenever He wants to do it.

> God was not obligated to create us, and He is not obligated to save us.

> Everything God does for us is an act of sheer, sovereign, amazing grace.

> Therefore, everything we are and ever hope to be is because of Him!

That thought should lead us to praise and worship every day we draw breath! This second principle is not simply a statement of theology.

It's meant to be a crucial steppingstone in our spiritual life. First, you admit that God is God, and you are not. Then you confess your utter and complete need of God. Until you can say that from your heart, you are not even on first base in your spiritual journey. There are many places in the Bible that teach this truth. As I prepared this chapter, my mind was drawn powerfully to Psalm 100.

> **Psalm 100** *"Shout for joy to the Lord, all the earth. Worship the Lord with gladness; come before him with joyful songs. Know that the Lord is God. It is he who made us, and we are his; we are his people, the sheep of his pasture.*
>
> *Enter his gates with thanksgiving and his courts with praise; give thanks to him and praise his name. For the Lord is good and his love endures forever; his faithfulness continues through all generations."*

Many years ago, this psalm was sung to a tune called 'the Old Hundredth.' Today we know the tune better as the 'Doxology.' The Hebrew text calls it, "A psalm for giving thanks." Even though there are many thanksgiving psalms, this is the only one specifically titled that way. It is sometimes called the *"Jubilate,"* which means *"O be joyful."* In Old Testament times, the Jews used it as part of the Temple worship. These simple words have blessed the hearts of God's people for nearly 3,000 years.

Psalm 100 has two stanzas and each is centered around God. We are to give thanks and praise the Lord because: He is God (verses 1-3), and He is good (verses 4-5).

Verse 3 says, *"Know that the Lord is God."* Older versions say, *"Know that the Lord, He is God,"* which makes it even more pointed. This acknowledgement of God's sovereignty leads to three corporate responses:

We shout for joy (verse 1), we serve the Lord with gladness (verse 2a), we sing with joy (verse 2b). Then there is a statement of ownership and assurance in verse 3b: *"It is He who made us, and we are His; we are His people, the sheep of His pasture."* Some versions say, *"It is He who made us, and not we ourselves."* I actually prefer that translation because it emphasizes that there are no self-made men or women. All that we have was given to us by God.

This leads us on to visible, public thanksgiving and praise: *"Enter His gates with thanksgiving and His courts with praise; give thanks to Him and praise His name"* (Psalm 100:4).

The design of the tabernacle and the temple allowed for large courtyards where great crowds of people would gather. The psalmist here exhorts the people to come into that courtyard singing and openly praising God's name. It's almost as if God is saying, *"You want to meet me? You can. Start singing a song and I'll meet you on the second verse."*

Part of the emphasis is surely meant to be that Israel would publicly praise the Lord. As the pagan nations watched from a distance, the public, loud, joyful worship of the Israelites would send a clear message to the watching world: *"These people know and love their God."*

I don't think it's out-of-place to suggest that we should be bolder and more public in our praise. Last weekend there were millions of Australians celebrating the winners of various football games played across our nation. Tens of thousands of people packed into different grandstands and shouted themselves hoarse as thousands more watched on via television. At the end of the season, people will decorate their homes, cars and workplaces with the colours of their team. There will be dancing in the streets and thousands will not make it to bed that night if their team wins!

If people can celebrate to that extent over a bunch of guys running around on the grass passing, kicking and scoring points with a piece of leather, how much more should we openly celebrate our great and wonderful God? We should be praising the Lord on the streets, in the parks, in the classrooms, in our jobs, in our offices, in our neighborhood, and with our friends and loved ones. While we don't need to be pushy or offensive, we shouldn't be silent either. A silent Christian is a contradiction in terms! Now we are certainly not the most reserved and inhibited people, by any means, but I think it is fair to say that we could all manifest the joy of the Lord a little more in our lives and our communities.

This great psalm then ends with these reassuring words: *"For the LORD is good and his love endures forever; his faithfulness continues through all generations"* (Psalm 100:5).

Because God's love endures forever, it has no beginning and no end. Before time began, God was the eternal Father of love. And since God is eternal, His mercy extends as far into the future as the mind can conceive … and then infinitely further. God's love and faithfulness will endure for ever and ever and ever! It never runs out, is never exhausted, and when you feel you have used up your allotment, you discover that there is an infinite river flowing from God's throne.

God's love is not like the weather. It does not change with the seasons. And it does not depend on you or on anything you may do. There is nothing you can do to make God love you more and there is nothing you can do to make Him love you less. His mercy is so great and His love so free that it is truly infinite and everlasting. We see God's love and mercy most clearly at the cross. Fix your eyes upon the blood-stained cross of Calvary.

Gaze upon the dying form of the Son of God. There you will find grace unmeasured, mercy undeserved, and love beyond measure. No changes in us or this whole universe, however great, can produce any changes in God. All things are moving according to His divine plan. There are no mistakes with the Lord. You may think otherwise, but it's not true. You may say, *"All things are against me,"* but it's not so. All things are *for* you - but you may not yet see it. God is ordering everything for the best.

The final phrase in Psalm 100 is: *"through all generations."* It literally means *"from generation to generation."* Exodus 20:6 tells us that God shows His love to *"a thousand generations"* of those who love Him. Since a biblical generation is 40 years, this means God's love lasts at least 40,000 years. Since this promise was given to Moses at Mt. Sinai approximately 3,500 years ago, we may safely conclude that God's faithful love will continue at least another 36,500 years. That is to say, in 3,500 years we are not yet even 10% of the way through a thousand generations!

Of course, I doubt God was using this figure literally - but it's not purely figurative either. It's a way of showing us that God's love and faithfulness go far beyond any human understanding. Suppose we line up a grandfather, a father, a son, a grandson, and a great-grandson before us. This text tells us that what God is to the grandfather, He will be to the father. What God is to the father, He will be to the son. What God is to the son, He will be to the grandson. What God is to the grandson, He will be to the great-grandson and on it goes across the centuries. Generations come and go, one after the other. Only God remains forever.

This is our hope at the edge of death. This is why we rejoice as we bury our dead. Nothing of God dies when a man or woman of God dies.

We need not fear death because a Christian is immortal. We do not know how far we have to go until we reach the end of our earthly road. But this we know - that road is paved with God's love and faithfulness; we need never be afraid.

Many years ago, a wise old man encouraged me to pray the last sentence of the Lord's Prayer every day: *"Yours is the kingdom, yours is the power, yours is the glory, forever. Amen."* (Matthew 6:13).

That's a part of the Lord's Prayer that most of us don't even think about, but it is absolutely crucial. We pray *"yours is the kingdom"* because we know that the kingdoms of the earth will give way to the kingdom of the Lord Jesus Christ. We pray *"yours is the power"* because we do not give up in the face of difficult trials but instead live in faith that the Lord has a purpose, and He will give us whatever we need to face the challenges of each day. We pray *"yours is the glory"* because we have chosen to live for God instead of for the praise of men.

We need to pray that way because we are all kingdom builders who love to operate in our own power and for our own glory. I therefore encourage you to say to the Lord every day: *"Not my kingdom but yours, Lord. Not my power but yours, Lord. Not my glory but yours, Lord. And not just today or tomorrow but forever. Amen."* If we pray like that, and if we live like that, we'll stay out of the kind of trouble that could destroy us. As we wrap up this chapter, let me draw all this together into three simple statements:

1) God owns everything; we own nothing.

Our problem is that too often we don't feel our need until things aren't going well. But we need God just as much when we have a million dollars as when we are flat broke.

We need God just as much when our health is good as when we are struggling with disease. We need the Lord. We need Him desperately. We need Him more than we will ever truly know.

2) Our lives are broken because of sin.

Sin has messed everything up. The whole world groans and travails because of sin. Nothing works right; things break; children are shot as they sit in their classrooms; marriages disintegrate; promises are broken; laws are violated; and terrorists fly airplanes into buildings. The world is broken, and we are broken. Like Humpty Dumpty, nothing we do can put us back together again.

3) If God doesn't help us, we're sunk.

That should be obvious by now. I love how David puts it in Psalm 34:6, *"This poor man called, and the LORD heard him; He saved him out of all his troubles."* Take that verse backwards and you come to a wonderful truth. If you want to be saved, the Lord must hear you. But to be heard, you must call on the Lord. But only a 'poor' man or woman calls on the Lord. Those who think of themselves as self-sufficient, have no need for God, so they never call on Him. Only the 'poor' call on God and are heard and saved and delivered. That's what Jesus meant when He said, *"Blessed are the poor in spirit for theirs is the kingdom of heaven."* (Matthew 5:3)

Blessed are the poor in spirit, and those who mourn, and the meek who confess their own weakness. They will embrace the power, reality and confidence of the kingdom of heaven, they will be comforted, and they will one day inherit the earth. Blessed are the needy … Blessed are the desperate … Blessed are the broken … Blessed are the weak … they will find the Lord!

If the first principle of Christian living drives us to our knees - the second principle keeps us there until we cry out for mercy. It is a great advance in the spiritual life to bow before the Lord and say, *"Oh God, I need you. I can't do this myself. Please help me."* No one who has cried out to the Lord like that has ever been turned away. And when we finally get off our high horse and cry out to God, then (and only then) are our prayers answered and God is glorified. But you'll never know until you see this for yourself. I can preach all day long, but it will have no effect until those listening admit how much they need God.

> ***You will never know if Jesus is all you need,***
> ***until Jesus is all you have.***

> ***When Jesus is all you have,***
> ***then you will know Jesus is all you need.***

If you are weary; if you are tired; if you are discouraged; if you need a fresh start; if you know your life is going nowhere; if you want your sins forgiven; if you want to know God - then drop whatever you are doing and run to the cross! Run to the cross! Don't delay; don't put it off; and don't make any excuses. Drop everything and run to the cross of Christ and may God give you faith to believe as you lay hold of Jesus and hold on tight.

God doesn't need us - but we desperately need Him!

3. GOD'S BIDDING IS GOD'S ENABLING

The third principle of Christian living is actually a promise: *God's Bidding is God's Enabling.* Or more simply put, God will never require anything of us which He is not ready and willing to empower and enable in us. We know that religion sets unachievable goals which we can never meet. The Old Covenant did the same. Under the New Covenant, in Christ and through Christ, God *empowers* us to become all that He *desires* us to become!

This is a wonderful promise and word of hope for all those who find themselves face down in the dust with nowhere else to turn. This principle brings us to the very heart of the gospel. If we understand this, then we know why the gospel truly is *Good News!*

Once upon a time, in a faraway place, God appeared to Abraham and told him to take his son Isaac to the region of Moriah and sacrifice him there as an offering to the Lord. Just an average day in the life of a patriarch!

The words of Genesis 22:2 emphasize the close bond that existed between father and son: *"Take your son, your only son, Isaac, whom you love ..."*

Now there are many questions we'd like to ask at this point, foremost among them being, why would God ask a father to sacrifice his own son? Isn't the very request a violation of God's nature?

If there was a discussion between Abraham and God, or if Abraham hesitated when he heard the command, it's not recorded in the text. All we know is that the next morning Abraham took his son and his servants and set out to do exactly what the Lord required.

When they got to the region of Moriah (which is modern-day Jerusalem), he said to his servants, *"Stay here with the donkey while I and the boy go over there. We will worship and then we will come back to you"* (Genesis 22:5).

You've got to wonder what he was thinking and how much he understood. Hebrews 11:19 indicates that he thought that God would raise his son from the dead. Somehow Abraham looked beyond the immediate circumstance and found faith to believe that the God who would take his son from him could also give him back.

As they walked along together, father and son, Isaac asked a question that must have broken Abraham's heart. *"Father, I see the wood and the fire, but where is the lamb for the sacrifice?"* With an even greater flash of insight, Abraham replied, *"God Himself will provide the lamb for the burnt offering, my son."* (Genesis 22:8).

Across the centuries, Christians have seen in these words a prefiguring of the death of Christ on the cross. Abraham (representing God) places the wood (representing the Cross) upon Isaac (representing Jesus Christ). It is the father offering his son freely and without complaint, just as God the Father offered Jesus for the sins of the whole world.

Somehow Abraham understood something far deeper than this event. When he said, *"God himself will provide the lamb,"* he was pointing not simply toward the altar on Mount Moriah, but to a greater sacrifice to be offered at the very same location almost 2,000 years later when God provided the Ultimate Lamb - Jesus Christ - for the sins of the whole world. Whether Abraham was conscious of this or not is unknown, but he was certainly part of a very powerful prophetic event.

When they reached the right spot, Abraham built an altar of stones and placed the wood on top of it. Then he bound Isaac and placed him on the wood. I don't know what words passed between father and son at this point, but I doubt that much was said. What does a father say to his son in a moment like that? What does a son who loves and trusts his father say as his hands and feet are bound?

Then came the moment of truth. Abraham raised his hand and prepared to plunge the knife into the breast of his son. At that very moment, not one second sooner and not one second later, God spoke to Abraham: *"Do not lay a hand on the boy. Do not do anything to him. Now I know that you fear God, because you have not withheld from me your son, your only son"* (Genesis 22:12).

Again, the timing is crucial. As Abraham looked up, he saw a ram caught by its horns in a nearby thicket. I am sure he ran to get that ram before it freed itself and got away. With the same knife that he would have used to take his son's life, he slit the ram's throat, drained the blood, laid it on the altar, set the wood on fire, and offered the ram to the Lord.

Only one detail remains. Abraham called the place *"The Lord will provide."* The traditional English rendering of the Hebrew is *Jehovah Jireh.* Abraham meant, *"Here is the place where God saw my need and provided the ram to meet my need."*

As we read this story, it's too easy to focus on Abraham's amazing faith. But the real hero of the story isn't Abraham. The real hero is God! As great as Abraham was, God was greater. He gave Abraham a seemingly impossible demand and then He provided what Abraham lacked - a morally righteous way to meet that demand. God did what only God could do. He supplied what Abraham needed to fulfill God's will.

What God wanted all along was not the death of Isaac, but Abraham's unquestioning submission and obedience. But it had to happen the way it did in order for Abraham to demonstrate his faith and for God to demonstrate His grace.

That happened early in the history of the Old Testament. Several hundred years passed and then God spoke to Moses on Mount Sinai and gave him the law that would guide the people of Israel. If you have read Leviticus, you know that God gave Moses instructions regarding various offerings and sacrifices.

Blood, death and sacrifice then dominated the life of God's people for centuries – but all this was meant to point to something else – to God's ultimate plan. From the very beginning, God was always looking towards something better. Hebrews 10:1 tells us that the law was a "shadow" of good things to come.

In a sense, the entire sacrificial system was meant to prepare the Jews for the day when John the Baptist saw Jesus and exclaimed, *"Behold, the Lamb of God, who takes away the sin of the world!"* (John 1:29). What an amazing statement that is.

First of all, He is God's Lamb sent from heaven to earth. If we offer a sacrifice, the best we can do is to offer a literal lamb or a goat or to round up a bull and bring it to the priest. Animal blood was all we could offer. When God offers a lamb, that 'lamb' is His own Son. He is the perfect sacrifice. All those animals the priests put to death were meant to point directly to on Lamb; Jesus Christ.

Secondly, He is God's lamb offered for our sins. The word translated "takes away" is used elsewhere in the Bible for the rolling away of the stone that sealed the tomb of Jesus. When our Lord died on the cross, He "rolled away" our sins once and for all.

Thirdly, He is God's lamb who rolls away the sins of the whole world. Here's an amazing truth. The blood of Jesus is so powerful that it is sufficient payment for the sins of the whole world. Anyone, anywhere, at any time is forgiven through Christ. There are no barriers that stand between you and eternal life. Jesus paid the price for it all. From the godliest person to the vilest – Christ secured forgiveness for the whole world!

Why? Why does God do this? Well, there is something in God that causes Him to provide whatever we need to meet His righteous requirements and that "something" is grace. Let me make this very simple: Here is the whole gospel in three simple statements. Are you ready? If anyone asks you what the gospel is, try telling them this: God said, *"Do this."* We said, *"We can't. God said, "I know. I will do it for you."*

God requires perfection because God is perfect. We cannot meet that standard. So, God sent His Son to live that perfect life on our behalf and to die the death we deserved. God requires payment for sin because God is holy. We cannot make that payment without ceasing to exist which was never an option for a God Who loves us and created us to be in fellowship with Him for eternity. So, God sent His Son to pay that price, in full, on our behalf.

God requires righteousness. But all we have to offer are the filthy rags of our soiled self-righteousness. So, God sent His Son, Who took our sin so that we might be clothed with His perfect righteousness. God requires a blood sacrifice for sin. But we cannot meet that demand and stay alive.

So, He sent His Son to die in our place, shedding His blood, paying the price, bearing our burden, offering Himself as the final sacrifice for all sin – past, present, and future.

Without blood, without death, without sacrifice, no one can come into God's presence. But we weren't even qualified to die for ourselves, much less for anyone else. We weren't perfect, or pure, or unblemished. Sin had marred every part of us. We were blemished and unacceptable.

If God doesn't do something <u>for</u> us, we are sunk. His holiness demanded a perfect sacrifice. His love sent us His Son. In this we see the glory of the gospel. God says, *"You must."* We say, *"We can't."* God says, *"I will."* So He sent His Son from heaven to earth to do for us what we could never do for ourselves. This is why the Bible says what we have sung often: *"salvation belongs to our God."*

Everything starts and ends with God. Salvation doesn't start on earth and rise to heaven. It starts in the kingdom of heaven and comes to earth through Christ. <u>God</u> takes the initiative. <u>God</u> makes it happen. While you were dead in your sin, <u>God</u> made you alive in Christ. That's why the most famous verse in the Bible begins with the words: *"For God so loved the world that He gave ..."* (John 3:16).

You'll never understand why Jesus came until you grasp the meaning of those words. Jesus is God's gift to the whole human race - entirely undeserved. A gift given in spite our sin. A gift many despised and rejected. A gift that was brutally crucified. But even His crucifixion was part of the gift from God. Through His death came our eternal life.

God knew we were dead in our sins ...
   ... *so He sent Christ to give us life.*

God knew we were His enemies ...
   ... *so He sent Christ to make us His friends.*

God knew we were like orphans ...
   ... *so He sent Christ to bring us into His family.*

God knew we had no hope …

    … so He sent Christ to give us a home in heaven.

God knew we were poor …

    … so He sent Christ to make us rich.

God knew we were enslaved…

    … so He sent Christ to set us free.

God knew we were afraid to die…

    … so He sent Christ to die and then raised Him
      from the dead.

God knew we had nothing…

    … so He gave us everything in Christ.

What God required from us, God gave to us. What we needed, He provided. His bidding was His enabling. But wait, there's more … not a free set of steak knives … something much better! God knew we needed guidance, so He gave us the Bible. God knew we needed wisdom and power, so He gave us the Holy Spirit. God knew we needed encouragement, so He gave us brothers and sisters.

God placed us *"in Christ."* At this point all those wonderful words of the gospel come right into play: words like *salvation, forgiveness, grace, mercy, love, peace, hope, eternal life, redemption, substitution, propitiation, reconciliation, adoption, justification, regeneration,* and *glorification*. <u>All</u> of this is given to us *freely* in Christ. New life. New hope. New heart. New mind. New standing. New position. New name. New power. New direction. New destiny. All of it is ours, all of it is free, all of it comes to us as a gift from God through Jesus Christ our Lord.

Religion says, *"Do this and live."* God says, *"I have done it all for you – now receive it in faith and <u>really</u> live!"*

Right there you find the whole gospel in a nutshell: It's <u>do</u> vs. <u>done.</u> As simple as that. All religion is based on 'do' – (works). You go to heaven because of what you do: Give money. Go to church or to the synagogue or the mosque. Pray toward Mecca. Light a candle. Pray all night. Keep the feast days. Give alms to the poor. Offer a sacrifice. Keep the Ten Commandments. Be baptized. Follow the Golden Rule. Be a good neighbour. Don't get in trouble. Obey the law. Stay out of jail. Be courteous, kind and forgiving. Try harder. Do your best. Follow the program. Live a good life.

In looking at that list, it's important to note that many of those things are good and right and noble. There's nothing wrong with them. But the problem with the 'do more, try harder' mantra of religion is that you can never be sure you've done enough or tried hard enough! And if somehow you finally manage to do enough, how do you know that you won't blow it all tomorrow by one stupid sin?

Religion is evil. God hates religion! Religion is what held God's children captive until Jesus came to the rescue and smashed religion and drove out the religious spirits. The Christian faith is built upon the foundation of grace alone. Sometimes you will hear the phrase "free grace" but that is a nonsense statement. It's like saying "wet water." As opposed to what? Dry water? **If it's not free, it's not grace.**

If you have to *do* something, anything at all, to earn it or merit it or deserve it, it's not grace! The whole difference comes down to this: Christianity is based on what Christ has done for us – before we were even born – before we committed our first sin – before we even knew Christ existed. Religion is based on what we do ourselves.

Let me make the point even sharper here with a question. Are you satisfied with what Jesus did for you on the cross?

If you are, then all you have to do is rest in Him for your eternal salvation and rest in Him for an abundant, fruitful life. If you are not satisfied with what Jesus did, then you will end up trying to do something to add to His finished work on the cross. That is when religion is birthed in you and that is why it's so evil and arrogant, because the truth is, **<u>God</u> is satisfied with what Jesus did.**

Religion tells us that we have to do more to add to what Jesus did. Jesus said, *"It is finished."* Religion says, *"but there's more to do .. and <u>we</u> have to do it!* So, is Jesus enough to take you to heaven or do you think you've got to add something to what He did?

Let me close this chapter by explaining what all that means: Because of the work of Christ, we now <u>have</u> full forgiveness for <u>all</u> our sins. Not only that, we have the assurance that when we leave this world, we will be fully in heaven. We can say with confidence that even the worst sinner is a recipient of God's amazing grace. The door to heaven has been opened by the death of God's Son. Everyone comes through that one door marked *"Enter by grace alone."*

How then shall we live? Well, if God has provided <u>all</u> that we need, then we must reach out and receive <u>all</u> that He offers – every day! If we have truly experienced God's grace, then we will respond with profound gratitude. God has done it <u>all</u>. He has made a way for lost sinners to be forgiven. He found us, He saved us. He redeemed us. He gave us new life, and He ushered us into heaven.

When that truth really hits our hearts, we will give thanks to God every single day. I beg you in Jesus' name: come to the cross. Lay hold of the riches that are yours in Christ Jesus. Lay aside the rags of your own righteousness and receive the pure white robes of the righteousness of Christ.

Hold out your hands and He will fill them with every spiritual blessing. All that God has promised is yours for the asking. Would you like the water of life? Come and drink all you like. It's yours and it's free, flowing from the throne of grace. Just think about what is yours, through Christ:

> *He forgives with no payment whatsoever.*
> *He forgives all our sins once and for all.*
> *He promises complete reconciliation.*
> *He gives you assurance of your salvation.*
> *He makes you His son, His daughter.*
> *He places you in Christ.*
> *He gives you access to God, 24 hours a day.*
> *He gives you a new heart and a new life.*
> *He gives you a home in heaven.*
> *He promises to raise you from the dead.*
> *He promises that you will be like Him.*
> *He promises you will reign with Him forever.*

All of this is yours *in Christ*. Does that not lift your spirit? Does that not make you want to sing? Does that not make you want to dance? Remember this one truth. What God requires - God supplies. God's bidding is God's enabling. All that we need, we find in Christ.

Praise God for His amazing grace!

4. WHAT WE SEEK, WE FIND

Now we are turning a corner in our exploration of the ten key principles of Christian living. This fourth principle takes us into the practical realm. It tells us that *"What we seek, we find."* Those five words challenge us at the level of personal motivation. As I was preparing this chapter, I was struck by how much the Bible has to say about seeking and finding, especially seeking and finding God. Here are just a few examples:

Deuteronomy 4:29 *"But from there you will seek the LORD your God, and you will find Him if you seek Him with all your heart and with all your soul."*

1 Chronicles 28:9 *"As for you, my son Solomon, know the God of your father, and serve Him with a loyal heart and with a willing mind; for the LORD searches all hearts and understands all the intent of the thoughts. If you seek Him, He will be found by you ..."*

2 Chronicles 26:5 *"He sought God in the days of Zechariah, who had understanding in the visions of God; and as long as he sought the LORD, God made him prosper."*

Psalm 27:8 *"When You said, 'Seek My face,' My heart said to You, 'Your face, LORD, I will seek.'"*

Isaiah 55:6 *"Seek the LORD while He may be found, call upon Him while He is near."*

Jeremiah 29:11-13 *"You will seek Me and find Me, when you seek Me with all your heart."*

Matthew 6:33 *"But seek first the kingdom of God and His righteousness, and all these things shall be added unto you."*

Luke 11:9 *"Ask, and it will be given to you; seek, and you will find; knock, and it will be opened to you ..."*

Hebrews 11:6 *"But without faith it is impossible to please Him, for he who comes to God must believe that He is, and that He is a rewarder of those who diligently seek Him."*

This list is just the tip of the iceberg. This whole concept of 'seeking God' is an enormous biblical concept that speaks to our motivation; our priorities; how we spend our time; the goals we set in life; and our spiritual growth (or the lack thereof). Let me summarize what these verses are saying with three very simple statements:

1. Everybody seeks something

By nature, we are all seeking people. Some people seek money; others fame; others pleasure; others self-validation; others seek sexual fulfillment; and others seek worldly power … everybody is seeking … all the time. The tragedy of our time is that so many people are wasting their lives seeking what can never satisfy.

I confess I watched a little of the Rugby League grand final last year – just a little. But I was interested to see and hear all the hype leading up to the start of this one game. I can remember the commentator describing this one match as 'The ultimate game.' I pondered that statement for a while and thought of all the time, energy, money and effort which was focused all year towards this one day, this one game.

If you want to see what seeking looks like, then watch those final few weeks of matches leading up to this 'ultimate game.' Then I started to smile as I thought to myself, *"If this is the Ultimate Game, why do they play it again next year?"* That's exactly the way things are in this crazy world. You climb to the top of the heap only to discover that next year you've got to start all over again. Nothing in this world ever truly satisfies us.

2. There's an easy test to find out what you seek in life.

Here's a simple test to help you discover what you truly seek in life. This test is absolutely foolproof. You tell me how you spend your time and your money, and then I will tell you what you are seeking.

You can say anything you like; you can attend church services and look religious; but your time and your money don't lie. Show me your calendar and your bank account transactions and I will show you what you truly seek and what you truly value.

There are millions of people on this planet who are a lot like the Professor on Gilligan's Island. The Professor knew how to turn banana peels into diesel fuel, and he could take algae and make chocolate fudge, but did you notice that he never got around to fixing the hole in the boat so they could get off the island?! Many of us are the same. We spend our life learning to do amazing things that don't really matter – all the time ignoring the hole in our boat - and that's why we are stuck where we are! We are seeking the wrong things.

3. Whatever righteous thing you seek in the spiritual realm, you can have it, if you want it badly enough.

"Blessed are those who hunger and thirst for righteousness, for they will be filled." (Matthew 5:6). This is one of the most stupendous promises in the whole Bible. If you are hungry and thirsty for the righteousness that God provides, you will be filled. If you want righteousness, you can have it. Whatever righteous thing you desire in the spiritual realm, you can have if you want it badly enough.

Abraham Lincoln once declared that *"most people are about as happy as they want to be."* This is so true. Along those same lines, I would say that most of us are about as close to God now as we want to be. We have about as much joy as we want and about as much peace as we want.

We are the way we are, because that's the way we want to be. Either we're happy that way or we've accepted that this is who we are and we're not going to change.

For the most part, you are where you are right at this point in your life because that's where your desires have taken you. If you were really hungry for something better from God, then you would have something better from God.

- *If you want it, you can have a closer walk with God.*
- *If you want it, you can have a better marriage.*
- *If you want to, you can do God's will.*
- *If you want to, you can witness for Christ.*
- *If you want to, you can learn to pray.*
- *If you want to, you can grow spiritually.*
- *If you want to, you can walk in the Spirit.*
- *If you want to, you can become a mighty man or woman of God.*
- *If you want to, you can change deeply ingrained habits.*
- *If you want to, you can break destructive patterns of behaviour.*

What we seek, we find. This is true in every area and realm of life. Unless we seek, we will not find. And what we seek, be it good or bad, we eventually will find. Our problem stems from the excuses we make. We don't change and we don't grow and we don't seek God and we stay the way we are, because that's pretty much the way we want to be. We've learned to live with mediocrity and either we think things will never change or we're happy the way things are. I can think of three excuses that keep us trapped in that rut of mediocrity. The first is the excuse of self-pity. Self-pity is the greatest enemy of spiritual growth. As long as we mope around feeling sorry for ourselves, we can't get better. And we'll be stuck right where we are.

The second excuse is the *"I'm trying"* excuse. Whenever we say, *"I'm trying,"* that's just an excuse for not doing what we say we want to do. We can excuse any sort of non-performance by saying, *"I'm trying."* In one of the Star Wars movies, Yoda tells Luke Skywalker to use his powers to do something that seemed impossible. *"I'll try,"* said Luke. *"No!"* said Yoda. *"Try not! Do or do not. There is no try."*

- *You've either got a drinking problem or you haven't.*
- *You're either reading the Bible or you're not.*
- *You're either paying off your credit cards or you're not.*
- *You're either losing weight or you're not.*
- *You're either using drugs or you're not.*
- *You're either forgiving that person who hurt you or you're not.*

Saying *"I'm trying"* is just a weak excuse to take the pressure off yourself. You get credit for doing something that you're not really doing. It's a way of deceiving yourself into thinking you've changed when nothing has changed. If I was an alcoholic in an AA meeting and I said, *"I am trying to quit drinking."* I would hear the mantra: *"Trying is Lying."* It is lying both to myself and to anyone else who heard it. If I want to lie to myself that is one thing, but I would be told that I should really have the decency not to waste the time of the group by lying to them.

If you're on the receiving end of that comment, it's really tough to hear. But we have to learn that the real solution always lies in admitting, *"I am powerless to change myself,"* but God *"can and will change me if I truly seek Him."*

The third excuse is simply saying, *"I'll never change"* or *"I can't change"* or *"I don't want to change."* If that's your bottom line, then I have absolutely nothing for you and you may as well put this book down right now! Until you really <u>want</u> to change, you are doomed to stay exactly the way you are right now. If that attitude resides in more than a few people in a church congregation, then that church is already dead and just needs a good burial.

The entire Christian life is about change, transformation, and renewal. We are called by God to a lifetime of change. He never, ever wants us to 'remain as we are' – He is always wanting to transform us more into the image of Christ. God wants to mold us and shape us in such a way that the life of Christ within us permeates our very being and transforms every area of our lives!

So, let me ask you this question: are you a God-seeking person? It is not enough to be religious or simply committed to attending church events. As good as that may be, it's not the same thing as seeking God with all your heart, soul, mind and strength. I want to challenge you in this next week to do something very difficult but potentially life-changing. I want you to go to someone who knows you well and ask them this question: *"Am I a God-seeking person? When you look at my life, do you see the qualities in me of a person who truly seeks God?"*

If you want a really good test, try going to a friend or relative who is not involved in the church at all and doesn't share your faith in God - and ask them! You may be surprised at how readily they answer. Those outside the church may not understand the intricacies of our faith, but they know the difference between someone who seeks God and someone who doesn't. In some cases, I think unbelievers are less easily fooled than believers. Since they don't focus on the outward trappings as much as we might, they can spot a God-seeking heart, even if that's not what they would call it.

People who don't know the Lord instinctively recognize a person who truly knows God and seeks God passionately. This is a question a Buddhist can answer, or a Hindu, or a Muslim, or a Jew, or even someone who isn't spiritual at all. Go ahead. Ask them, *"Am I a God-seeking person?"* They will tell you the truth as they see it.

So, if you want a God-seeking heart, where should you begin? I have four suggestions:

1. Admit your need. You cannot change until you admit that you need to change. If you are happy the way you are, then none of what I write here will matter to you. But if you are just tired of turning banana peels into diesel fuel while there's still a hole in your boat, then listen to what the Spirit is saying to the church today and admit your need.

2. Cry out to God for help. The Bible is full of stories of men and women crying out to God throughout history and God was there for every single one of them! If you need the Lord, cry out to Him today. Seek Him with all your heart and you will find Him.

3. Surround yourself with God-seeking people. You know who they are. God-seekers aren't hard to spot. Find some friends who truly seek the Lord and glue yourself to them. Go where they go, do what they do. Follow their example. Eventually one of two things will happen. Either they will drive you nuts, and you will leave them or they will rub off on you and you will become a God-seeker too!

4. _Wait on the Lord._ This is a hard discipline for most of us to master. Our message to God is usually, _"Give me patience Lord, and give it to me now!"_ We want spiritual maturity, and we want it by the end of this week! We're not accustomed to waiting patiently on the Lord.

Our whole culture is not good at waiting for anything at all. But waiting has so many positive benefits. The very act of waiting re-orients our hearts and increases our longing to know the Lord intimately. As we wait and as we pray, we become like the deer panting for the water. Our soul grows hungry to know the Lord.

The great mystic Thomas a Kempis once said, _"Seek God, not happiness."_ We have it all backwards in our broken world. We seek happiness and hope to have God thrown in as a bonus, and we end up with neither! The paradox of the gospel is that when we truly seek God, we find Him, and we end up with true happiness (i.e. deep fulfillment, lasting joy and abundant life). But it takes years for many of us to figure that out, and some of us never get this. To the very end, we pursue earthly happiness and our own agenda, and we wonder why our life leaves us frustrated and disillusioned.

I want to wrap up this chapter with a final thought. Jesus' appeal is always personal. He never says, _"Come and join the church"_ or _"Come and be baptized"_ or _"Come and give your time and money."_ He simply says, _"Come to <u>me</u>."_ Then Jesus says, _"You will be filled,"_ He means, _"You will be filled with Jesus Himself!"_

- _If you are hungry, come and eat of the Bread of Life._
- _If you are thirsty, come and drink of the Water of Life._
- _If you are weary, come and find rest in Him._
- _If you are guilty, come and embrace His forgiveness._
- _If you are far from God, come back home again._

The French philosopher Pascal was the one who first said that there is a _"God-shaped vacuum"_ inside every human heart. Since nature abhors a vacuum, if we don't fill it with God, it will be filled with something else.

So many of us have filled our hearts with the 'junk food' of this world. No wonder we are unhappy. No wonder we jump from one job to another and from one relationship to another. No wonder we stay the way we are. We're trapped in the pit of a thousand excuses. We'd rather have misery and pain than risk it all on Jesus.

Many centuries ago, Augustine explained both the problem and the solution when he said: *"O God, you have made us for yourself, and our hearts are restless until they find rest in you."* You will never be happy until you put God first in your life, and you can never do that until you surrender your life to Jesus Christ.

In the kingdom of heaven, everything begins with a seeking heart! Salvation begins with a hungry heart. If you are tired of the life you've been living, you can make a new start. In the kingdom of heaven, you will find what you truly seek.

5. GOD RESPONDS TO FAITH

Let's begin by reviewing the first four key principles of the Christian life:

1. *He's God and We're Not.*
2. *God Doesn't Need Us*
3. *God's Bidding is God's Enabling*
4. *What You Seek, You Find*

Each of these four principles cover a major area of our relationship with God and leads us to a personal response. Now the fifth principle moves us into a whole new area: *God Responds to Faith.*

Faith is one of the most prominent words in Christianity. Sometimes the word refers to an entire belief system, such as 'the Christian faith' or 'the Islamic faith' or 'the Jewish faith'. In other contexts, it refers to a body of doctrine, as in 'Keep the faith.'

Mostly, however, faith refers to our personal response to God. The 'faith' of this fifth principle is not religion or a set of doctrines, but rather our daily, moment-by-moment trust in God. When our faith is active, it releases the reality of Christ in us and through us.

Hebrews 11:6, in most translations, says that *"without faith it is impossible to please God."* This is one of those verses in the Bible that I really wish had never been written – not like this anyway. When it is read in context with the whole gospel, I don't have a problem with it at all. However, on its own, which sadly is how it's quoted 99% of the time, it has too often become fuel for the performance-based religion which God hates with a passion.

This whole notion of 'pleasing God' is so misunderstood by fallen humans like us. As soon as we come into this world we are programmed to do more and try harder to please our parents, our school teachers, our friends, our employers, our pastor and our fellow Christians. We want please those people so we perform for them.

When we read a verse like this, we can instinctively try and treat God the same way we treat the humans around us. But it doesn't work! It never will and that's not what this verse in Hebrews 11 really means anyway.

The trouble is, the way it is written and translated, we easily interpret: the more faith I have, *the more pleased God will be with me.* The only way you could believe that is if you have failed to truly understand the gospel at all!

"Without faith it is impossible to please God" is one of those *"the sun rises in the east"* statements in Scripture. That is what appears to happen, but the reality is very different. The sun does not rise anywhere, does it? No, the earth is what moves in relation to the sun - but it *appears* the sun rises in the east.

Hebrew 11:6 simply means that without faith you will never fully embrace and know God. No matter how religious you may be, if you do not have faith, you cannot experience the fullness of God in Christ.

The fact is, God cannot ever be 'pleased' with you outside of Christ. Nothing you do will ever be good enough to please God. You are sinful, fallen and alienated from God and you can stack performance upon performance and not come close to pleasing God – not in a million lifetimes! So, brace yourself for the good news now:

God is already pleased with you in Christ.

If you are in Christ, then God is 100% pleased with you because of the perfect performance of Jesus against God's holy law – which has been credited to you as righteousness – and its a free gift from God. So, the only way you can truly enter into God's pleasure is to have faith in the finished work of Christ in you. I so wish the writer of Hebrews had said that here, so millions of people could not take this verse out of context and kick the guts out of the gospel!

In my opinion, Hebrews 11:6 should read: *"Without faith in the finished work of Christ in you, it is impossible to truly know God, Who is pleased with you."*

Through faith in Christ, we respond to and encounter God. You can be baptized; go to church; give money; attend Sunday School; read your Bible; fast and pray; sing in the choir; lead a ministry or even become a Pastor or missionary … but if you don't have faith in Christ Who is in you, you will not embrace the power and reality of the kingdom of heaven – you will not truly experience God.

Faith is also not a one-time experience when we first come to Christ. It is a moment-by-moment attitude; a complete orientation; a lifestyle. The same faith we exercise to believe and receive the grace of God and our salvation in Christ, is the faith which carries us from day to day as we journey deeper into the kingdom of heaven. That's why the Bible says, *"The righteous shall live by faith,"* and in Romans 1:17 we read that the gospel reveals a righteousness that is *"by faith from first to last."*

The whole Christian life is a life of faith. We embrace our salvation by faith, we are kept by faith, we walk by faith, endure by faith, rejoice by faith, serve by faith, love by faith, sacrifice by faith, pray by faith, worship by faith, and we obey by faith.

So, what is faith? In the Bible there's no clearer instruction on faith than Hebrews 11. Most of us know this as the 'Faith Hall of Fame.' Here we have a list of Old Testament heroes, most of them introduced with the phrase "by faith."

By faith Abel … (v. 4)
By faith Enoch … (v. 5)
By faith Noah … (v. 7)
By faith Abraham … (v. 8)
By faith Isaac … (v. 20)
By faith Jacob … (v. 21)
By faith Joseph … (v. 22)
By faith Moses' parents … (v. 23)
By faith Moses … (v. 24)
By faith the people … (v. 29)
By faith the walls of Jericho fell … (v. 30)
By faith Rahab the prostitute … (v. 31)

The writer says he doesn't even have time to mention the individual exploits of *"Gideon, Barak, Samson, Jephthah, David, Samuel and the prophets."* (Hebrews 11:32). They and all the other heroes of the faith are summarized here:

> **Hebrews 11:33-35a** *"Who through faith conquered kingdoms, administered justice, and gained what was promised; who shut the mouths of lions, quenched the fury of the flames, and escaped the edge of the sword; whose weakness was turned to strength; and who became powerful in battle and routed foreign armies. Women received back their dead, raised to life again."*

That's a wonderful list and we can all think of the great biblical heroes who did these things. But that is only part of the story:

Hebrews 11:35b-38 *"Others were tortured and refused to be released, so that they might gain a better resurrection. Some faced jeers and flogging, while still others were chained and put in prison. They were stoned; they were sawed in two; they were put to death by the sword. They went about in sheepskins and goatskins, destitute, persecuted and mistreated - the world was not worthy of them. They wandered in deserts and mountains, and in caves and holes in the ground."*

Who are these poor, unenlightened souls? What have they done to deserve such punishment? The writer simply calls them "others." They are "others" who lived by faith. These men and women who endured such torment were living by faith just as much as Noah, Abraham, Moses or Joshua. Their faith was not weaker.

If anything, their faith was stronger because it enabled them to endure incredible suffering. They are not "lesser" saints because they found no miracle. If anything, they are "greater" saints because they were faithful even when things didn't work out right. Then comes this summary statement of the whole list:

Hebrews 11:39 *"These were all commended for their faith."*

As we step back and study this list, three factors quickly emerge. First of all, though these individuals are widely separated by time and space (and by personality and individual achievement), they are joined by one common factor: What they did, they did by faith in God.

Secondly, living by faith often meant moving against the prevailing tide of public opinion. Noah built an ark; Abraham left Ur; Moses rejected the wealth of Egypt; and Joshua marched around Jericho like an idiot.

The same principle holds true today. If you decide to live by faith, you will definitely stand out from the crowd, and you may face opposition and ridicule.

Thirdly, Hebrews 11 demonstrates that the life of faith is not supposed to be a rare gem. It's easy to look at Enoch or Noah or Joseph or Moses or David and say, "I could never do that." Down deep in our hearts, we have believed a lie that the life of faith is restricted to a few 'special' people. We think we could never qualify to have our names added to the Hebrews hall of fame. But that's the very reason this chapter is in the Bible, so that we would know that these are ordinary men and women who did extraordinary things simply because they had faith in an extraordinary God. They are made of the same stuff as us.

The life of faith is within the reach of every believer because faith is a gift from God – freely given to everyone who wants it. You don't have to be special, talented or particularly bright … you just have to believe and receive. That's the way you get anything and everything from God – believe and receive – it's all by faith.

Hebrews 11:1 offers us a concise definition of faith: *"Now faith is the assurance of things hoped for and the conviction of things not seen."* I personally prefer the traditional rendering because it is more picturesque: *"Now faith is the substance of things hoped for, the evidence of things not seen."* The word 'substance' is an unusual word that refers to the 'essential nature' of things. It was sometimes used of the foundation of a house and beyond the New Testament it was used for the title deed to a property.

So, faith is like the 'title deed' to things hoped for, things promised by the Lord. It is the confident assurance that what we hope for will someday come to pass.

The word 'evidence' refers to legal proof in a courtroom. So, faith is proof to the soul that enables us to see things that cannot be seen by the naked eye. Through the eyes of faith, we 'see' what would otherwise be invisible.

Now there's a sense in which living by faith requires a good measure of holy discontent. Not human discontent, which is always self-focused, but holy discontent which is God-focused. You've got to want something that you don't have in order to have faith because faith always deals with things 'hoped for.' If you are already experiencing everything you need, want or desire; and if for you all the promises of God have already become a reality for you, and if you've reached a state of spiritual perfection; if all your prayers have been answered and if all your loved ones are saved and serving the Lord; if there is no lack anywhere in any area that you can see, then you don't need faith - because you're living fully in heaven already and you just don't realize it. If you are completely satisfied with your life and the world around you, then you can skip this chapter altogether because it doesn't apply to you.

But as long as we still have sick people, lonely people and damaged people; as long as marriages keep breaking up, and children suffer; and as long as the killing continues, and our leaders disappoint us; and as long as there is hatred and violence and prejudice and all manner of evil in the world - we will need faith because the "things hoped for" have not yet come to pass.

What, then, is faith? Think about these three words:
Believe, See, Do.

> Faith *believes* what others do not believe.
> Faith *sees* what others do not see.
> Faith *does* what others do not do.

True faith is never passive. True faith moves us to act; to do; to try; to build; to attempt; to expand; to say "no" to sin and "yes" to righteousness; to join up; to speak out; to move forward; to dare to dream beyond our means; and to walk around Jericho again and again … no matter how stupid we look or feel until finally *those walls come tumbling down.* That's faith!

I once heard someone say that faith is *'outrageous trust in God.'* I like that a lot. Outrageous trust is what you have when you build an ark hundreds of miles from any body of water. Outrageous trust compels you to leave your home not knowing where you are going because some unknown God spoke to you. Outrageous trust sends you into the Elah Valley to face Goliath with nothing but a slingshot and some stones. Have you ever been in a situation where you needed an outrageous trust in God?

Let's pause for a moment and take a closer look at the case of Moses. The heart of his story is found in Hebrews 11. Consider Moses, who could have become Pharaoh one day but by faith he left Egypt, not fearing the king's anger; he persevered because he *"saw Him who is invisible."* He found the strength to persevere and endure forty years in Midian because he *"saw him who is invisible."*

Moses gave up the riches of Egypt in order to join the motley band of Hebrews who were so hated by the Egyptians. And he found the strength to endure the persecution because he *"saw Him who is invisible."* That's one of the most remarkable and revealing statements in the entire Bible.

How do you 'see' an invisible person? God was invisible and yet Moses 'saw' him. How? By faith. Moses had faith which gave him spiritual sight and he saw the God who is invisible. The Egyptians didn't see. But Moses did.

That's what faith can do. So, what did Moses see? The text says he was *"looking ahead"* to his reward. Moses knew there were two worlds and he could choose to live by the values of either one. There was the world he could see, the world of Egypt, the world of the senses, the world of money, power, sex, pleasure, fame, self-gratification, the world of military power and brute force. Then there was (and is) another world. That's the invisible world of the spirit, the realm of God, the Lord Jesus Christ, the angels and the saints. It's a world that is ruled by righteousness and entered only by grace and embraced only by faith.

Now here's the kicker: Those who live for this world will have the reward of this world when they die. That is: all that they lived for will die with them. They will be buried or incinerated and have nothing substantial to show for their time on planet earth. But those who live in this world but also embrace the eternal kingdom of heaven, have an entirely different experience.

Like Moses, they may suffer in the short-term, but they will enter into *"the joy of the Lord,"* and those who live in this earthly kingdom by the values of the kingdom of Heaven will have deeper joy and greater satisfaction even while they are rejected and ridiculed by those around them. Somehow Moses saw all this. He figured out that it wasn't worth it to live for Egypt. For Moses, there was only one choice. He would suffer with the people of God. End of discussion.

So, the question is, in which world do you want to make your mark? If you want to make it big here in 'Egypt', good luck. Go for it. You will have your reward, and you won't be happy when you get it. If you want to live for the kingdom of God, you can, but it might cost you something in the meantime.

Now there is so much more I could say about faith, but we need to move on to other key principles so I will leave it there for now. However, just in case the spirit of legalism wants to invade your head while you are pondering the issue of faith, let me emphasize four things about faith.

- Faith is a gift from God.
- The object of our faith is always God Himself.
- Faith is not a task, a duty, a work, a requirement, or a discipline.
- Faith is the moment-by-moment orientation of our heart towards God.

With that understanding of faith, I want you to read Hebrews chapter 11 a couple more times as soon as you can. As you do, remember this: the same gift of faith bestowed upon those 'heroes of faith' you are reading about is being held out to you today, and every day by God.

If you want to experience the fullness of the kingdom of Heaven and see the life of Christ within you transform your thinking, feeling and living … then I encourage you to accept that gift from God and keep on accepting it day after day after day. For without faith, you will miss so much of what God is waiting to do in you and through you.

6. NO PAIN, NO GAIN

The sixth key principle of Christian living is one you may not like much – but it really is just as important as the rest: *'No Pain, No Gain'* simply means there's no growth without struggle. Because we live in a fallen world, nothing works the way it's supposed to. Sin has stained every part of the physical universe and sin has deeply infected humanity. Things break. Our bodies wear out. We grow old and die. People kill each other. Marriages break up. Our youth get hooked on drugs or alcohol or sex. Babies are born with defects that cannot be corrected. Priests and teachers and family members molest children. Our friends disappoint us and we disappoint our friends … and the list goes on!

As the old jazz song from the 1930's says, *"Into each life some rain must fall."* This sixth principle brings us face to face with a reality that some Christians would rather not talk about. The Christian life is not easy. Yes, Jesus said that His yoke was easy, and His burden was light, but He also talked about taking up your cross daily, denying yourself, and following Him. He also said that the world hated Him, and the world will hate us too. There's nothing particularly easy about that. Jesus just offers to take the load for us – He never said he would remove the struggle or pain.

That being said, the Christian life is still the best life there is - because it's the only true life. To know Christ is to know God, and to know God is to know eternal life. Jesus said that anything you give up will be redeemed many times over in this life, and more in the life to come. The paradox is this: If you follow Christ, you must lose your life to save it. You must let the cross do its job in you every day to discover the power of the resurrection. You must die to yourself to find abundant life. You must reckon yourself dead to sin, in order to experience the fullness of life in Christ.

None of this is particularly easy to do. If you think it's easy, that's only because you haven't taken the Bible seriously. In Romans 7, Paul speaks of a 'war' going on in the inner life of the believer.

Romans 8:13 exhorts us to "put to death" the deeds of the flesh. Galatians 5:17 tells us that the flesh and the Spirit are continually at war with each other.

Christians traditionally have spoken of three great enemies we face: the world, the flesh and the devil. The world is 'out there' and all around us. Our 'flesh' loves to answer the call of the world, and " ... *the devil roams like a roaring lion, seeking whom he may devour.*" (1 Peter 5:8).

No wonder the Bible says that *"through many tribulations we must enter the kingdom of God."* (Acts 14:22). And that's why Paul told Timothy to *"share in suffering as a good soldier of Christ Jesus."* (2 Timothy 2:3). The most sung hymn of all time, *Amazing Grace*, contains a verse that teaches this same truth:

> *Through many dangers, toils and snares,*
> *I have already come.*
> *'Tis grace has brought me safe thus far,*
> *and grace will lead me home.*

Truly, there are many dangers, toils and snares which come our way as we journey through life with Jesus. But this principle reminds us that those difficulties can be for our spiritual benefit. Spiritual growth is not instant or easy.

There are no shortcuts to maturity in our faith journey. Football coaches have said this for generations: *No pain, no gain.* So here are four truths that help us think clearly about our trials:

1) *Because we live in a fallen world, bad things happen to all of us.*

2) *We don't have control over many things that happen to us or to those around us.*

3) *We do have complete control over how we react and respond to all that happens.*

4) *Our response to our trials largely determines our spiritual growth - or lack thereof.*

If I was to expand this sixth principle more, it would say: *Struggle in the Christian life is inevitable, lifelong, and ultimately beneficial.* We encounter God's grace through our trials in ways that would not happen if the trials had not come in the first place. It takes a mature Christian to understand this principle, and ironically, it is this principle that helps us mature in our faith.

Many years ago, a mentor of mine told me: *when hard times come, be a student, not a victim.* The more I have pondered those simple words, the more profound they seem to be. Many people are professional victims, always talking about how unfair life is.

A victim says, *"Why did this happen to me?"* A student says, *"What can You teach me through this Lord?"* A victim looks at everyone else and cries out, *"Life isn't fair."* A student looks at life and says, *"What happened to me could have happened to anybody."*

Victims feel sorry for themselves and have little time for others. Students focus on helping others so that they have no time to feel sorry for themselves. Victims beg God to remove the problems in life so that they might be happy. Students have learned through the problems of life that God alone is the source of all true happiness.

In the book of James we find many practical guidelines that will help us be students and not victims when hard times come our way. Here is one of them:

James 1:2 *"Consider it pure joy, my brothers, whenever you face trials of many kinds."*

James is reminding us that sooner or later (probably sooner) we will all face trials of various sorts. The word "face" has the idea of falling or stumbling over a problem. Picture someone driving down the highway in a convertible. The top is down, the music is blaring, and the driver is having a great day. Not a problem in the world; not a care or a concern. Suddenly there is a bump, a jolt, and the car comes to a sudden halt. What happened? The car hit a massive pothole and snapped the axel. Suddenly the happy journey is all over. Life is like that for all of us.

No matter who we are or where we live, trouble may just be a phone call away. A doctor may say, *"I'm sorry. You've got cancer;"* the voice may inform you that your son has just been arrested; you may be fired from your job without any warning; someone you trusted may start spreading all kinds of lies about you; your husband or wife may decide they just don't want to be married to you anymore.

The list is endless because our trials are 'multi-coloured' and 'variegated' (the meaning of the Greek word translated 'of many kinds'). How, then, should we respond to these hard times which can suddenly come upon us?

James offers what appears to be a strange piece of advice: *"Count it all joy."* That sounds so odd that you wonder if he's serious. *"Joy? Are you nuts? Do you have any idea what I've just been through?"* It does sound rather idealistic, if not downright impossible.

I confess to be being bothered by this many years ago so I decided to check it out in the Greek. Guess what the word translated as "joy" here really means? Joy! No help there. So I decided to check out some other translations. One version says, *"Be very glad"* and another says, *"Consider yourselves fortunate."* That didn't help either, so I turned to my trusty J. B. Phillips translation, hoping for some light (if not a way of escape). This is how he handles verse 2:

"When all kinds of trials and temptations crowd into your lives … don't resent them as intruders but welcome them as friends!"

I stopped searching at that point. I got the message. I think it's the exclamation point at the end that does it for me. It's not just *"welcome them as friends,"* which would be hard enough, but *"welcome them as friends!"* To me it sounds like he's shouting with excitement, like he's welcoming long-lost friends to his home.

As I've pondered this issue more, and considered my own difficulties with this concept, the thought occurs to me that *"counting it all joy"* when troubles come is just not a natural response for any normal human being. If we want a natural response, we can talk about anger or despair or complaining or getting even or running away. It just isn't natural to find joy in hardship.

But that's the whole point! James isn't talking about a natural response. Clearly, he is talking about a supernatural response - made possible only by the Holy Spirit Who enables us to see and to respond from God's point of view.

I suggest then, that *"counting it all joy"* is a conscious choice we make when hard times come and it's probably a choice we'll have to make again and again. To do that, we'll have to take the long view of life, to understand that what we see is not the final chapter of this story.

If we can make the choice to view life that way, then we will always trust God when the trials come, knowing that nothing catches Him by surprise and even though God may not have 'sent' this trial our way, He certainly knew it was coming and only God knows how to use the nasty stuff in life to perfect us and transform us into the image of Christ, which is God's will for us all.

But here's a very practical tip for you. Don't trust your feelings! When those you love are in great pain; when you face senseless tragedy or loss; when friends turn against you; when life tumbles in around you - your feelings won't be an accurate guide. You won't 'feel' joyful or grateful or full of trust. You are quite likely to be filled with a whole bag of negative emotions.

Don't judge your circumstances by your feelings. Judge your circumstances by the Holy Spirit and by the Word of God. When you do that, you begin to look at your trials very differently. Seeing things God's way doesn't cancel your trials and it doesn't turn them into non-trials, but it does transform your response and attitude to those trials. You will view them differently because you believe that God intends, through them, to give you a great blessing that may not come any other way.

I think our main struggle with this passage in James comes because we completely misunderstand the word "joy." In our contemporary vocabulary, the word is virtually a synonym for happiness. Joy to many people speaks of a day at the beach or a great party or a New Year's Eve bash.

To us, joy means the absence of all pain. But that's not what the Bible says it is. Joy comes from God – it is one of the fruits of the Holy Spirit in us.

Joy emerges from a deep satisfaction that comes from knowing that God is always in control, even when my circumstances seem to be out of control. The key to joy is knowing that God is God and we are not and that, as out of control as our life may feel, God has not taken His hand off us – not even for a second. If you know that, then you can be satisfied at a very deep level, even while you weep over what is happening around you or to you.

We also need to understand that excessive grief can be very selfish and if we turn inward for too long, it's not healthy at all. Too often we can make some disappointment, loss, grief or tragedy, an excuse for shirking our other responsibilities.

There is nothing more selfish than sorrow, nothing more absorbing, if we let it. Serving others and God is our best comforter next to the promise of God's Holy Spirit. And so, how can we go on when sorrow has paid us a visit? What shall we do when tragedy strikes, and we feel like giving up? Here are five suggestions:

> *Remind yourself of the promises of God*

Talk to yourself and forcibly call to mind the promises of God's presence, His comfort, His divine care, and His declared purpose to mould you into the likeness of Christ. In the darkest hours, the promises will not come easily. You must do whatever it takes to feed your own soul with the Bread of Life.

> Give thanks for all the good things

There are many times when thanksgiving seems impossible and sometimes even inappropriate. But even if you cannot give thanks for 99% of what is happening, focus on the 1% you clearly see and give thanks to God for that. There are always blessings to be seen – ask God to show them to you.

> Refuse to give in to bitterness and despair

Here I speak of the conscious choices of the heart. Too many times we speak as if we were involuntarily overwhelmed and had no choice but to be bitter, angry, and hostile. Or we had no choice but to give up our faith in God. Better that we learn to say, *"I could give in to anger, but by God's grace I will choose a higher road. I could turn away from my Lord, but I will consciously choose to turn to Him."*

> Choose to believe in God

That means exactly what it says. Believe in God! Believe in His goodness. Believe in His love. Believe in His kindness. Faith is a gift from God, but it's our choice to exercise that faith and believe in the goodness of God. If you want to believe, you will believe, and all of heaven will be cheering you on!

> Make up your mind to move forward

Grief is appropriate and proper, and it is healing and even beneficial, but after grief has done its job, we must move on. The past is gone, and we can't go back. Don't even try. You can't live in yesterday. The voice of God calls us onward toward tomorrow – He never calls us back – that's Satan's strategy! Let me share with you a simple principle which I call the First Law of Spiritual Progress. It goes like this:

> I can't go back

> I can't stay here

> I must go forward

Even if we want to go back, we can't. We also can't stay where we are now. God's call is always forward, always moving out by faith into an unknown future.

This is not easy, but it must be done, and when we do it, we will discover a well of joy springing up to refresh our souls as we move forward with the power of the Lord.

James 1:3 *"Because you know that the testing of your faith develops perseverance."*

Every word of this verse is crucial. The phrase *"you know"* does not refer to head knowledge but to heart knowledge, the kind gained by years of experience. Some things we learn from books, others we learn in the 'School of Hard Knocks.' This lesson comes from daily life. God wants to put our faith to the test. The word *"testing"* here refers to the process by which gold ore was purified.

In order to separate the gold from the dross, the ore was placed in a furnace and heated until it melts. The dross rises to the surface and is skimmed off, leaving only pure gold. That's a picture of what God is doing to us during our *"fiery trials."* We all must do some *'furnace time'* sooner or later, and some of us will spend an extended time in the furnace of affliction. But the result is the pure gold of Christ's own character emerging in us.

Job spoke of this experience when he declared of the Lord, *"He knows the way that I take; when he has tested me, I will come forth as gold."* (Job 23:10). What is God trying to do when He allows His children to go through hard trials and deep suffering? First, God wants to purge us of sin and to purify us in Jesus Christ. Second, God uses suffering to test and strengthen our faith. Will you still be obedient to God in the darkness? Will you serve God when things aren't going your way? Will you hold on to the truth when you feel like giving up? Third, God uses times of difficulty to humble us. When things are going well, we tend to get puffed up about our accomplishments.

But let the darkness fall and we are on our knees crying out to God, a great place to be! Fourth, God definitely uses hard times to prepare us to minister to others. He comforts us so that we may comfort others. I know many Christians whose greatest ministry has come from sharing with others how God helped them through a time of crisis. Fifth, I believe God uses hard times to prepare us for a new understanding of His character. In the furnace, we discover God's goodness in a way we had never experienced it before.

Until your faith is put to the test, it remains theoretical. You never know what you believe until hard times come. Then you find out, for better or for worse. Until then, your faith is speculative because it's untested. You can talk about the kingdom of heaven all you want, but you will only discover whether you really believe in that kingdom when you stand by the casket of someone you love.

God's great design is to produce *"perseverance."* The Greek used word here is sometimes translated as *"endurance"* or *"steadfastness"* or *"patience."* In the book of Revelation, this word describes the faith of those brave saints who would not take the Mark of the Beast. So, it describes a certain kind of 'battle-tested' faith that stands up under enemy fire and does not cut and run. William Barclay notes that in the early church, the martyrs gained the respect of unbelievers because in the moment of death, they had this quality. To the very end, they died with their faith intact. Of them it was said, *"They died singing."*

> **James 1:4** *"Perseverance must finish its work so that you may be mature and complete, not lacking anything."*

There is a process involved in our trials that leads to an end result. Perseverance requires work and faith and hope and dogged determination to hold on to our faith even when the world seems to be disintegrating around us.

Perseverance says, *"I will not give up, no matter what happens or how bad life may be. I will hold on because I promised and because I believe the Lord has something in store for me."* The end result of such a gritty stubbornness is genuine spiritual maturity.

When trials have finished their work in us, we will not lack anything. If we need faith, we will have it. If we need hope, we will have it. If we need love, we will have it. If we need any of the nine-fold fruit of the Spirit (Galatians 5:22-23), it will be produced in us.

The great danger is that we try to short-circuit the process by running away from our problems. Eugene Peterson (The Message) translates part of this verse this way: *"Don't try to get out of anything prematurely!"* That's good advice; but it's not always easy to follow that advice.

So, when trials come (and they will come to all of us), we can't always know why things happen the way they do, but we can know that God is always at work in our trials for our blessing and growth and for His glory. To say that, is to say nothing more than the words of Romans 8:28. For the children of God, *"all things"* do indeed *"work together for good."* Sometimes we will see it - often we will simply have to take it by faith - but it's true whether we see it or not.

When hard times come; when trials fall upon us; or we seem to fall upon them; when the slings and arrows of outrageous fortune knock us to the ground, what should we do? Remember these two words. *Pray* and *stay*.

Don't run. Don't hide. Don't shake your fist at God. Don't start arguing with the Almighty. And certainly don't waste time trying to make excuses or empty promises. Just pray and stay.

Pray: Seek God's face. Spend time with the Lord. Listen for His voice. Ask God, *"What are you trying to teach me? Speak, Lord, and I will listen to your voice."*

Stay: Wait. Be patient. Don't try and rush God. Refuse to run away. Affirm by faith that God is at work even though He seems invisible, and your life seems chaotic.

The Christian life is not an easy life and any representations to the contrary are false. There is an abundant life to be had, and there is spiritual victory and there is joy in the Lord and the filling of the Spirit, but those things don't come in spite of our trials. Most often they come through and with and alongside our trials. But in the midst of every trial, we are totally responsible for our choices and there are many:

- Joy or bitterness.
- Forgiveness or anger.
- Trust or unbelief.
- Faith or fear.
- Love or hatred.
- Kindness or malice.
- Temperance or self-indulgence.
- Gentleness or stubbornness.
- Mercy or revenge.
- Peace or worry.
- Hope or despair.

God is ready, willing and more than able to empower our right choices … but He will not be a guest at our pity parties; He will not indulge our wound-licking inward focus; He cannot empower choices which hurt us more and hurt those around us. His love will never fail us, regardless of our choices, but in the midst of every trial we face, the voice of God is calling to us, *"Come to me … don't run from me – and we will get through this together."*

7. WE ARE CALLED TO DIE

John 12:24-26 *"I tell you the truth, unless a kernel of wheat falls to the ground and dies, it remains only a single seed. But if it dies, it produces many seeds. The man who loves his life will lose it, while the man who hates his life in this world will keep it for eternal life.*

Whoever serves me must follow me; and where I am, my servant also will be. My Father will honour the one who serves me."

Late one night a jeep drove into the clearing. Four men with machine guns jumped out. Inside they handcuffed the schoolteacher and pastor of the local church. He and a friend were then forced into the jeep. They rode along the rugged road until they reached the bridge. There they pushed the pastor out.

Knowing what was going to happen he asked permission to write a few words in his diary. He noted the time, the date, and the events which were now transpiring. Then he simply wrote: *"We are going to heaven."*

Then he was told to walk over to the bridge. As Pastor Yona walked, he sang:

There is a happy land where saints in glory stand,
There's a land that is fairer than day,
And by faith we can see it afar:
For the Father waits over the way,
To prepare us a dwelling place there.

His song ended with a burst of machine gun fire and his body tumbled off the bridge into the river below and yet another chapter was written in the extended Book of Acts.

On Sunday, April 8, 1945, the German pastor and theologian Dietrich Bonhoeffer was taken from a worship service he had just conducted for prisoners. Hitler's Gestapo took him to this concentration camp in Flossenburg, tried him for treason, and hanged him - only a few days before the Allied Forces liberated the prison camp. A medical doctor at the scene described Bonhoeffer's final moments:

"Through the half-open door in one of the huts, I saw Pastor Bonhoeffer, before taking off his prison garb, kneeling on the floor praying fervently to his God. I was most deeply moved by the way this lovable man prayed, so devout and so certain that God heard his prayer. At the place of execution, he again said a short prayer and then climbed the steps to the gallows, brave and composed. His death ensued after a few seconds. In the almost fifty years that I worked as a doctor, I have hardly ever seen a man die so submissive to the will of God."

Survival is a popular theme these days. We have a top rating T.V. show focused on a group of people in an isolated island or Australian bush country competing; working together; scheming; negotiating; forming secret pacts and alliances; eliminating all threats; all with the goal of surviving and getting one million dollars. The show is called 'Survivor' and various versions of it have swept across the world with unprecedented success over the past decade. One of the top films many years ago was *Castaway*, the survival story of a postal service manager who spent years in isolation on a lonely tropical island. His only companion was a volleyball he named Wilson.

Survival is the most natural thing that we do. It is our most base instinct, the preservation of our most precious personal possession – our lives! But when it comes to following Jesus Christ and knowing the life that He has promised us, the quest for survival creates a real conflict.

The desire for our survival and the quest to preserve our lives keep us at a mediocre level of living. It eats away at our beliefs and convictions in such a way that we find it easy to compromise and almost impossible to confront. The end result of this is spiritual stagnation.

The quest for survival affects our decision-making; it robs us of our effectiveness; it saps our passion, freedom, and joy in the Lord; it hinders our wholehearted obedience; and it robs us of the power and blessings of God. Survivors are insecure; they rely on things other than God. They won't take risks. Survivors are unwilling to pay the price. They are more concerned with maintaining the things they have. They want to protect their rights.

In all this concern for survival, however, there is probably no instruction as strange and as powerful as that of the Lord Jesus Christ and what He says in the above passage from John's gospel. Against this whole society-wide quest for survival at all costs, we have perhaps the greatest and most confronting key principle of the Christian life: *We are called to die.*

In John 12:24 we read that if we are to bear fruit for God, like a seed, and like Christ, we must die. Now when I am dead, I will not care what they do with my body. It will make no difference to me. I've been to a morgue, and I assure you that dead people aren't worried about money, possessions, pleasure, university degrees, popularity, fame, being understood, having their needs met, etc.

Why? Because they're dead! In Jesus' name understand this … someday when you are dead, you will be at home with Jesus and none of those things will matter … am I right? Well, that's the way it is now, too, if you have died already with Christ, which all Christians have.

Galatians 5:24 *"Those who belong to Christ Jesus have crucified the flesh with its passions and desires."*

Crucified means dead. So, in a profound sense I am dead on the earth and my life is hidden with Christ in God. (Colossians 3:3) It therefore doesn't matter what happens to me here on earth. Paul regarded himself to be a dead man walking. His life was no longer his to live as he pleased. If we are going to experience revival instead of survival, we must first accept that we are called to die!

When people lose a loved one, they not only hold a funeral service, but they often go to the grave and leave flowers in memory of the dead person. Doing this helps some people come to grips with the death that has occurred. It is part of the grieving process and grieving is just a process of letting go and dealing with the loss that has occurred.

Maybe that's what we should do as Christians. Let's hold a funeral service … acknowledge the death that has taken place, visit the gravesite of our old selves and leave some flowers. Stand there for a few minutes and then leave and move on from that point. Do whatever helps us come to grips with the reality that the person we used to be, has died … with Christ on the cross.

> **Galatians 2:20** *"I have been crucified with Christ and I no longer live, but Christ lives in me. The life I live in the body, I live by faith in the Son of God, who loved me and gave himself for me."*

The verb in this opening statement of Galatians 2:20 is in a particular form that means it's a 'done deal' with lasting effect. Our crucifixion with Christ has already taken place. We're not dual personalities living double lives.

You may say, *"But I don't feel crucified."* That's all right. Dead people don't feel dead. But you are crucified with Christ because God says so, whether you feel it or not.

This is why Paul could say his only boast was *"in the cross of our Lord Jesus Christ."* (Galatians 6:14). Paul rejoiced in the cross not just because it meant that his sins were paid for, but because the old Paul ... that old hate-filled persecutor of the church ... was dead and gone.

There is this strange thing called *"hating your life in this world."* (John 12:25). What does that mean? We might say, *"The one who would save his life must save it."* It seems obvious enough. But Jesus said, *"The one who would save his life must lose it, for only by losing it, can he save it for the life to come."* Jesus used a Hebraic saying of extreme contrasts. The key phrase is *"hating your life in this world."* It is a 'good' kind of hating. A kind of hate that is noble and essential. A hatred towards anything that would take the central place of Christ in our lives. It means, at least, that you don't take much thought for your life in this world.

In other words, it just doesn't matter much what happens to your life in this world. If men speak well of you, it doesn't matter much. If they hate you, it doesn't matter much. If you have a lot of things, it doesn't matter much. If you have very little, it doesn't matter much. If you are persecuted or lied about, it doesn't matter much. Whether you are famous or unknown, it doesn't matter much. If you are dead, these things just don't matter much.

There are some choices to be made here, not just passive experiences. You cannot enjoy the fullness of God's blessing without submitting to the Lordship of Jesus Christ in your life. Jesus says, *"follow Me."* Where to? He is moving into Gethsemane and towards the cross.

Jesus is not just saying: *"If things go bad, don't fret, since you are dead anyway."* He is saying, *"Choose to die with me. Choose to hate your life in this world the way I have chosen the cross."* This is what Jesus meant when He calls us to choose, or 'take up' the cross.

> **Luke 9:23-25** *"If anyone would come after me, he must deny himself and take up his cross daily and follow me. For whoever wants to save his life will lose it, but whoever loses his life for me will save it. What good is it for a man to gain the whole world, and yet lose or forfeit his very self? If anyone is ashamed of me and my words, the Son of Man will be ashamed of him when he comes in his glory and in the glory of the Father and of the holy angels."*

People did only one thing on a cross. They died. *"Take up your cross,"* means, *"Like a grain of wheat, fall into the ground and die. Hate your life in this world. And choose to die!"*

The word 'daily' shows that following Jesus means a daily dying, not just a once-for-all dying. Each day I should experience, in practice, what is true of me in my position in Christ. I am once and for all *"crucified with Christ"* (Galatians 2:20; 5:24) - that's my position; my life is *"hid with Christ in God"* (Colossians 3:3). Therefore, I must believe this reality and act on it and experience it by faith. That is what Paul says in this foundational passage:

> **Galatians 2:20-21** *"I have been crucified with Christ and I no longer live, but Christ lives in me. The life I live in the body, I live by faith in the Son of God, who loved me and gave himself for me."*

Over the years there have been some music groups exposed as frauds because they just lip-synch the words on stage and never actually sing live. Perhaps we can be the same.

Instead of lip-synching the Christian life, affirming our position, mouthing the right words, while still trying to survive, God wants us to 'life-sync' the Christian life. He wants us to imitate Him in death so that we can imitate Him as well in life.

So, what's the point of all this? Is it aimless masochism? No. It is the path of revival, true love, true life, and true worship. Let me remind you of some wonderful promises.

> *Our aim in dying is **fruit**:*

John 12:24 *"But if it dies, it bears much fruit."*

John 15:5,8,16 *"I am the vine, you are the branches. He who abides in Me, and I in him, bears much fruit; for without Me you can do nothing..."By this My Father is glorified, that you bear much fruit; so you will be My disciples..."You did not choose Me, but I chose you and appointed you that you should go and bear fruit, and that your fruit should remain, that whatever you ask the Father in My name He may give you."*

The apostle Paul tells us what this fruit is:

Galatians 5:22-24 *"But the fruit of the Spirit is love, joy, peace, longsuffering, kindness, goodness, faithfulness, gentleness, and self-control. Against such there is no law."*

Those who belong to Christ have crucified the flesh with its passions and desires. It is not pleasant to die, but you will never truly live until you do. Some Biblical scholars call this *"the exchanged life."* I like that. When I exchange my life for Christ's life, He expresses Himself in me through fruit. When I move, Christ moves. When I speak, Christ speaks. Perhaps more accurately put: when Christ moves, I move and when Christ speaks, I speak.

George Mueller lived in England several generations ago and he founded many great orphanages, maintaining them solely through prayer. He was extremely effective. When asked the secret of his effective service, he replied:

"There was a day when I died to George Mueller, his opinions, preferences, tastes and will; died to the world, its approval or censure; died to the approval or blame of my brethren or friends; and since then, I have studied only to show myself approved unto God."

> *Our aim in dying is **life**:*

> **John 12:25** *"He who hates his life in this world shall keep it to, life eternal."*

It was the great missionary Jim Elliot who once said, *"He is no fool who gives what he cannot keep, to gain what he cannot lose."* When you are always seeking your own life, you are actually dying. When you are dying, you are actually living! Stop trying to live the Christian life. Understand that the Christian life is the life of Christ. It's not your life, but His. Jesus is the only person who ever lived as we were designed to live … and HE STILL IS. So, in order for you to live the Christian life, Christ must live His life through you, while you get out of His way!

> **2 Corinthians 4:10-11** *"We always carry around in our body the death of Jesus, so that the life of Jesus may also be revealed in our body. For we who are alive are always being given over to death for Jesus' sake, so that his life may be revealed in our mortal body."*

We are guaranteed of life in the present. (v.26) He will be with us, wherever we are. We are guaranteed of life in the future. If you are with Him here, you will be with Him there as well!

2 Timothy 2:11-12 *"Here is a trustworthy saying: If we died with him, we will also live with him; if we endure, we will also reign with him."*

Paul is the great example of what it means to die.

> **Galatians 6:14** *"[Through] the cross of our Lord Jesus Christ ... the world has been crucified to me, and I to the world."*

> **2 Corinthians 5:14-15** *"For Christ's love compels us, because we are convinced that one died for all, and therefore all died. And he died for all that those who live should no longer live for themselves but for him who died for them and was raised again."*

But why did Paul say these things? For the sake of radical commitment to ministry:

> **Acts 20:24** *"However, I consider my life worth nothing to me, if only I may finish the race and complete the task the Lord Jesus has given me-the task of testifying to the gospel of God's grace."*

"I consider my life worth nothing to me." This is a classic statement of a dead man walking. This is an *"I don't have to survive,"* statement. What mattered to the Apostle Paul was finishing the work God had for him. No wonder Paul was such a change-agent in the early church. No wonder he was willing to stand before the Jerusalem council and say that the gospel was for the Gentiles as well as the Jews. No wonder he was willing to be the first missionary, and was willing to be killed for it.

The Apostle Paul didn't have to survive. No one could stop him. Those who didn't like some of the statements he was making on the council floor couldn't take away his position.

Paul didn't have a position to lose. Those who wanted him to quit preaching could throw rocks at him, but that had happened before, and it didn't stop Paul. He would have counted it a privilege to suffer for Christ. They could also threaten him with prison, but Paul could laugh and say, *"Which one? Can I go back to Rome? I was witnessing there the last time I was in prison. Maybe I could lead another prison guard to the Lord."* Or they could threaten to kill him. *"Would you? I have had such turmoil inwardly. I don't know whether I should stay with the saints or be present with the Lord; if you would just knock me off, that would take care of my dilemma."*

What could be done to Paul? Absolutely nothing. Why did Paul choose to live this kind of life? Was it so he could be independent? Was it so he could call his own shots? No - it was so he could *"finish the race and complete the task the Lord Jesus has given me-the task of testifying to the gospel of God's grace."*

I have been asking myself earnestly, and I want you to ask this with me now, what in me must die? What must die for my life and ministry to bear more fruit? It's a scary question. This is the big picture of what it means to be a Christian. I don't want you to get the impression that this word from the Lord is a little peripheral word. This word about dying and hating your life in this world is not a marginal word. It is a central word. This key principle of Christian living is really a KEY.

So, today let us soberly ask ourselves some questions: is my life a quest for survival or revival? Is there something that is hindering the fruitfulness of Christ in me - something that I need to die to? Is there something God is calling me to die to so that I might experience more fully my position in Christ; that I might see Christ more clearly and follow him more compellingly?

Am I striving against my very nature as a Christian by trying to keep alive something God has sentenced to death when I became a Christian? Are my weaknesses as a parent or a spouse or a disciple caused by something that needs to die in me - some old habit; some secret sin; some root of pride; some fear of looking silly; some desperate need for approval; some desire for wealth?

Can I speak Christ's and Paul's words as my own today? Do I even want to? These are tough questions indeed – but really important ones which God will help us process.

Let me leave you with these words by a Pastor who wrestled with all those questions and really did understand their implications for his life.

'When Christ calls a man, he bids him come and die.'
(Dietrich Bonhoffer)

8. WE LIVE IN TWO KINGDOMS

Thus far we have explored seven foundational principles which undergird and define the Christian experience: *He's God and We're Not; God Doesn't Need Us - But We Desperately Need God; God's Bidding is God's Enabling; What We Seek, We Find; God Responds to Faith; No Pain, no Gain; What God Starts, God finishes.*

These are foundational principles which we really need to grasp and never lose sight of. However, beneath (or behind) all of those principles, is a vital, central truth we also must understand and live out each day: *We live in two kingdoms.* This eighth principle is really just the fundamental reality of the Christian faith – but one which is not embraced by so many believers. So, I want to go over some ground I have covered many times in sermons and books over many years as we are reminded of this vitally important reality.

When you were born, you were born into this fallen world, the kingdom of this earth, the kingdom of Satan, as the Bible calls it. This is the finite, material, cause-and-effect world in which we see, taste, smell, feel and hear. It is the world which dominates our time and thinking most days. It is the natural world, the earthly realm.

This is the kingdom in which the vast majority of people in the world reside exclusively. Anyone who has not accepted the gift of God's grace, been born again, and experienced the reality of the Kingdom of heaven is only aware of this earthly kingdom. This is reality as far as they know now. However, you and I and the millions of others who are born again Christians, do not only live in this earthly kingdom. The Bible says that we have been born again into a new kingdom - the kingdom of heaven, the kingdom of God.

This is a supernatural kingdom, an infinite realm and the eternal, everlasting kingdom where Jesus Christ rules as Lord. Unlike this earthly, finite realm, the kingdom of heaven is not perceived by our five senses. It is not visible, tangible and able to be experienced in the same physical way. It certainly impacts this physical world and our physical bodies but it also transcends them. It is a spiritual kingdom which is perceived and experienced by that part of us we call our spirit.

That's why Jesus said to Nicodemus in John 3 that, "... *flesh gives birth to flesh but spirit gives birth to spirit ...*" and unless we are born again into this spiritual realm, we will not experience its wonder, glory or power. It will not be real to us. It will be an illusion that is talked about, preached about and sung about, by millions of deluded people called Christians. To one who has not been born again – their only reality is this earthly kingdom. So, let's look at the two kingdoms as they are right now.

When Jesus came to earth over 2,000 years ago, He ushered in the kingdom heaven - He launched a full-scale heavenly attack on the kingdom of this world – a kingdom ruled by Satan. Jesus' intent was to rescue everyone who had been taken captive by the enemy. Through the life, death and resurrection of Jesus Christ, the power, glory and reality of the eternal kingdom of heaven was released on earth.

So now everyone who believes on the Lord Jesus Christ, that is, literally those who believe *into* Jesus; step *into* His life and embrace His life (as their own), His death (as their own) and His resurrection (as their own), they are born again into the kingdom of heaven. That is, they experience a spiritual awakening. Their spirit is regenerated by God's Holy Spirit. They are given a new citizenship - only this one lasts forever and is not of this world.

They remain part of the kingdom of this world as long as they live and breathe here, but they are now also a part of the eternal, majestic, supernatural kingdom of heaven which is gradually overtaking the kingdom of Satan so that one day there will be only one kingdom, one reality, one existence - the kingdom of heaven.

When that eclipse is complete, Satan will be gone, sin will be gone, everyone will bow the knee to Jesus and all flesh will know the glory of the kingdom of heaven and all unholiness and sin will be removed for all time. Until then, you and I and all believers, live in that middle area where the two kingdoms clash - and I mean clash. This is light vs darkness; sin vs holiness; truth vs error; grace vs law; God vs Satan; right vs wrong; power vs impotence; glory vs shame – it's a spiritual war!

These kingdoms are diametrically opposed to each other and so living with this dual citizenship is not easy and it will always bring with it a degree of tension, pain, conflict and confusion. It's like we have a dual personality. It's like we are two people in one body. As wonderful as it is to be saved, redeemed and living in God's kingdom - it is also a daily battle. That is what happens when kingdoms clash. Like it or not, we are caught up in the greatest cosmic battle we could imagine – but, of course, it's a battle which Jesus has already won in His kingdom!

So, when we pick up the Bible and start reading it, to find help in working out our salvation; how we should live and move and act and react as a Christian; it is absolutely essential that we understand this dual kingdom reality. We need to know that there are certain things which have happened and are happening in the spiritual realm, in the kingdom of heaven, which are not yet fully realised or experienced in this earthly kingdom.

We have to realise that although God has secured our salvation over 2,000 years ago in this earthly timeline, we still have to deal with the realities of a fallen, sinful world where there are many cause-and-effect consequences. Let me explain this by giving you some examples.

Sin: In the Kingdom of heaven, your sins are completely forgiven. They have all been atoned for by Jesus. There is no punishment for your sins anymore. Way back in the Old Testament, God foretold the day when He would wipe away our sins and He did that through Jesus. Jesus atoned for your sin. He paid the price for it once and for all. Is there any sin in the kingdom of heaven? No. Are you in the kingdom of heaven? Yes!

So, in God's eternal kingdom – Jesus has taken away your sin. Yet you still have to live in the kingdom of this world where Satan reigns and tempts us and lures us and inhabits our fallen nature and so we still sin, don't we? 1 John tells us we are liars if we answer 'no' to that question! We still stumble and fall.

But our sin can never separate us from God. Our sin can never again have any bearing on our eternal relationship with God - that was secured by the blood of Jesus Christ in the kingdom of heaven. God does not hide His face from us because of our sin.

All those Old Testament verses about sin coming between us and God no longer apply to born-again believers. Our sin, with respect to our eternal relationship with God, has been taken away and the very code (the law) which defined our sin and which Satan used to accuse us, has been nailed to the cross, once and for all! God still hears our prayers when we sin. God still blesses us with gifts and power and fruitful ministry when we sin.

All that stuff unfolds in the kingdom of heaven where our sin is atoned for and taken away along with all punishment. Yet back in this earthly realm, sin is still sin and it's as ugly and destructive and horrid as it has always been. Sin will still hurt you. It may even kill you physically if it's bad enough. It will destroy relationships. It will hinder the spread of the gospel and affect the credibility of the church in the eyes of the world. It will cause others to stumble. It will lead little ones astray when they see it in us. It will open the door for Satan to march into our lives, re-armed by our sin, and brings his ministry of distraction, discouragement, deception and death.

Sin is horrible. Don't do it. Flee from all evil. Stand firm against the schemes of the enemy. Your soul may be secure in the kingdom of heaven and your relationship with God may be secure in Christ but if you yield to the evil in this world and allow sin to reign in you then you will be living in darkness all your days on this earth and you will have to wait until you die to experience the abundance and glory of the heavenly kingdom. So don't sin!

But please don't ever let anyone tell you that your sin has any effect on your eternal relationship with God from His perspective - because it doesn't. This is the gospel. This is the truth. And that is why they call it 'good news.' That is why they call it grace.

Oh yes, let me assure you that if you continue to let sin have its way you will *feel like* you are a long way from God; you will *feel* punished; you will lose *the experience* of His grace as you allow Satan to have more and more control.

But Satan is the one who accuses, not God. Satan is the one who brings guilt and shame back into your life. Satan is the one who convinces you that God can't hear you or bless you or use you because you are an 'unholy' vessel.

Therefore, in this cause-and-effect world, sin will still bring horrible consequences into your life. You will reap what you sow. But don't confuse this kingdom for the kingdom of heaven where you currently sit at the right hand of God dressed in the righteous robes of Christ. Let's look at another issue from this two-kingdom perspective.

Forgiveness: In the Kingdom of heaven our forgiveness is complete. All your sin has been forgiven. Because there is no calendar in heaven that means there is no past, present or future. Therefore, your sin has been forgiven - period! That means that in this earthly realm, all your sin has been forgiven through the death of Jesus on Calvary.

The sins of Abraham were forgiven in the wounds of Jesus thousands of years before Jesus entered time and space. The sins of your great, great, great grandchildren are forgiven in the wounds of Jesus years before they are even born. That is the reality of forgiveness in the kingdom of heaven, where is no beginning or end. If you are a resident of the kingdom of heaven, then all your sins are forgiven!

Yet here in this cause-and-effect earthly world, there are days when you and I might really *feel* condemned and not forgiven. Our *experience* can at times be very different to the *reality* achieved for us in Christ.

That's why when the writers and translators of the New Testament have Jesus saying that God will not forgive us if we do not forgive others, they're not talking about what happens in the kingdom of heaven. The only realm that you and I can impact by our actions and our inaction is this earthly kingdom.

Nothing that happens in the kingdom of heaven is ever dependent upon what you or I do or don't do.

Now let me assure you that in this world, if you harbour unforgiveness or bitterness in your heart then it will grow like a cancer and it will rob you of the experience of God's forgiveness in such a way that you may feel condemned. But it will not be God who condemns you; it will not be God who robs you of the freedom and glory and wonder of the experience of being forgiven and cleansed. It will be Satan, working through your tortured conscience, empowered by your own unforgiving heart. In Jesus name, I pray that you get this.

You cannot lose your eternal salvation by your actions. You cannot lose forgiveness by your actions. It is all wrapped up in the same wonderful free gift of God's grace. It is secured for you, signed with God's hand, in the blood of His own dear Son. It is finished. But here, while we still have to struggle in this fallen, broken kingdom as well, we need to be diligent and not give the enemy any foothold by not forgiving everyone, every time, straight away. Here is another example:

Holiness and Righteousness: In the kingdom of heaven, you are united with Christ, washed by His blood, clothed in His pure white robes, filled with His presence and therefore you *are* the righteousness of Christ and you are 100% pure and holy. You have to be - if you want to be in the presence of God. Do you understand that holiness and sin cannot occupy the same space any more than you can go forward and backward at the same time? It is simply not possible.

Therefore, as you approach the eternal throne of God in worship and prayer, you must be pure, white, stainless, holy and 100% righteous. What happens if you are not? You vaporise! You are burned up by the holiness of God. So how is that possible? His name is Jesus, that's how. Jesus did that for you.

Jesus is the reason you can pray. Jesus is the reason you can talk to God and hear God talk to you. Jesus is the reason you can climb up on your heavenly Father's lap and call Him daddy - because in the kingdom of heaven you are in Christ and in Christ there is no sin; in Christ there is no unholiness; in Christ there is no unrighteousness. You are in Christ; you are spotless in the kingdom of heaven.

In this earthly realm, we are still working at letting that holy nature permeate our fallen nature. In this earthly kingdom we pray, we worship, we help each other, we hold each other accountable so that the holiness that is ours in Christ is manifested more and more in our lives. Little by little, it overcomes the fallen nature in us, as the kingdom of light gradually eclipses the kingdom of darkness.

Spiritual Gifts: Take a deep breath - this one might stretch you! All of the spiritual gifts are in Christ and Christ is in you. Therefore, you possess the fullness of God in Christ, which obviously includes all the spiritual gifts. That's right - prophecy, healing, discernment of spirits etc. They are all there. So what about the Bible passages that say, *"To one is given this gift and to another is given that gift..?"* Well, that refers to the practical outworking of the gifts in this world.

This is where it helps to study a little Greek. In the original language in which the New Testament was written, that verse could just as easily be translated, *"In one is released this gift, and in another is released that gift."* An interesting alternative, I'm sure you agree, and it is actually a more valid and helpful translation.

No doubt you have heard many preachers talk about spiritual gifts through the analogy of an orchestra. I think it is an excellent analogy but I actually interpret that picture very differently to most.

Most bible teachers see each of us as one member of that orchestra, playing our one instrument and occasionally the really talented few might even play two instruments at different times. The conductor is Jesus and He determines which gifts operate by determining who He puts in His church. That's a great picture. However, I see the picture very differently.

I see Jesus as the whole orchestra and God the Father (through His Spirit on earth) as the Conductor. Now, because you and I are in Christ, guess what that means? It means each of us, as believers, has the entire orchestra within us all the time, because Christ is in us. The Conductor can then release particular instruments in us at particular times as He sees fit and at times, He may release half a dozen at once in some people.

The hard thing is, in this limited, finite, cause-and-effect earthly kingdom, we find that picture very hard to embrace and so we would rather walk by sight and revert to a far inferior view of spiritual gifts, thereby robbing the Church of so much power and effectiveness.

I could go on with many examples, but if you understand the essence of what I am saying then you will see this dual reality in everything you think, say and do. It will help you make sense of difficult Bible passages.

The conflict we so often experience in interpreting the Bible is that we fail to have this dual kingdom concept firmly embedded in our thinking and so we will take passages that refer to our eternal condition in the kingdom of Heaven and apply them to our daily lives in this world and get really frustrated and confused. Or we will take exhortations to live pure, godly lives and clean up our act and apply them to our lives in the eternal kingdom and end up with no assurance of salvation or forgiveness or anything else!

We really must understand what it means to live in both kingdoms every moment of every day. After a while it will make sense and a lot of things will start to fall into place. Our ability to deal with sin will be far greater when we know that God is not our accuser.

The quality of our love relationship with God will increase markedly when we are not trying to please Him with our behaviour or our performance against the law which has already been obeyed fully by Christ, for us.

Some of the most famous words of Jesus are also the most profound, in my opinion. I refer to what we have called the Lord's prayer. The opening words of that prayer sum up this entire chapter and if we recited those words a hundred times a day, just maybe we would start to see how we are really supposed to live.

Jesus gave us a model for prayer and a model for life when He said we should pray, *"Our Father, who art in heaven, hallowed be Your Name, Your kingdom come, Your will be done on earth as it is in heaven."*

I preached a whole series on three of those words and still today they send shivers up my spine every time I say, read or write them: YOUR KINGDOM COME. These are three of the most powerful words you could ever utter. What do they mean? The words that follow tell us. *"Your kingdom come"* literally means: *"Your will be done, on earth as it is in heaven."*

This is a prayer that asks God to speed up the eclipse of these two kingdoms. When we say, *'Your kingdom come,'* we are asking that the reality of the Kingdom of Heaven would become the reality in this earthly kingdom. In fact, we are praying that one kingdom will replace the other!

Just think about that for a minute. *'Your kingdom come'* means that holiness, righteousness, peace, forgiveness, security, salvation, discernment, love, grace, peace, etc. all increase … while sin, evil, condemnation, fear, anxiety, ignorance, hate and all things evil decrease.

When we pray for God's kingdom to come, we are asking that the reality of heaven will become our experience more and more here on earth. It means that our life which is dominated by the finite, the natural - along with sickness, poverty, weakness, ineffectiveness - will more and more be dominated by healing, abundance, strength, power and rich fruit that lasts into eternity.

That is what's happening right now across the world. The reality of the kingdom of heaven is forcefully advancing against the reality of the kingdom of this world. In both a physical and spiritual sense, the lame are walking; the deaf can hear; the blind are beginning to see clearly for the first time; the power and the glory and the honour and grace and mercy and presence of God which saturates heaven is flooding the earth. Let's check this again to make sure we know the truth . . .

Are there any sick people in heaven? No. Well start praying for the sick now. The power of God to heal is increasing every day. If you are sick, you should ask someone to pray for your healing. If you know people who are sick you should ask them if you can pray for them and don't stop praying and don't stop believing.

Are there any lost people in heaven? No. Well guess what? The kingdom of heaven is here in power and there are over 80,000 people every day coming into the reality of that kingdom across the world. The power of God is present to save and convince people of their need of Jesus.

Are there any demonised people in heaven? No. Well there are millions down here who need setting free. Satan has taken God's children captive and his power needs to be broken in this kingdom like it already is in God's kingdom. As you and I pray those words, *'Your kingdom come,'* and believe them - the demons will flee and prisoners will be set free right across this nation.

Throughout my ministry over the past 40 plus years, I have sat in services and meetings where the kingdom of heaven flooded the room in a way I cannot describe and the powers of darkness manifested in many people right across the auditorium all at once. There was screaming and yelling and cursing and then the power of the Holy Spirit packed those demons' bags and sent them out the back door in one massive purging and the peace of God fell on that place and healed people everywhere. In heaven there are no demons tormenting God's people and soon there will be none here either as God's kingdom comes and God's will is done here, on earth, as it already is in heaven.

Are there any lonely, hurting, abused or rejected people in heaven? No. Well let's pray that the reality of the kingdom of heaven comes to our city through you and me as we reach out to the hundreds of people around us every single day who go through life not feeling love or acceptance or grace from anyone.

Learning to embrace the fullness of the kingdom of heaven whilst residing in the kingdom of this world, is not only one of the greatest challenges facing believers today, it also happens to be the very means by which we will change the whole world in which we live! *"Your Kingdom come, Lord!"*

9. THE GOSPEL = JESUS + NOTHING!

You may have grown up in the Church or you may have come to faith later in your life. You heard the message of forgiveness of sin; the love and acceptance of God; eternal life in a new relationship with Him; and your heart was pierced by the Holy Spirit as you responded to what God had already done for you. You knew without any doubt that God is real. He is powerful. He is your gracious, loving heavenly Father. You were filled with joy and everyone around you knew it.

Then maybe you were taught, or it was implied, that if you wanted to go on from there – if you wanted to be a 'first-class' Christian and really see the blessings of God, then you needed to start adding disciplines to your life and very soon these disciplines became standards or rules by which you judged yourself and others. You were told that Jesus is the only way to the Father, but then you need to do *your* bit.

Now if you don't think you were exposed to that kind of teaching, praise God! But I can assure you that hundreds of thousands of others were, and some of them are no longer with us in this journey and they need us to bring them back to the true gospel message of 'Jesus plus nothing!'

Let me make it clear right at the outset - if you hear 'Jesus plus something' you are not hearing an improvement on the gospel; or a new version of the gospel; or even a distortion of the gospel; you are hearing the absolute destruction of the gospel, along with its integrity and its power.

When, by the revelation and power of the Holy Spirit, we have those 'extras' removed as rules or requirements, then the beauty, purity and power of the gospel will return to our hearts and lives.

That is the whole focus of all my teaching and writing over many years. That is God's calling on my life. That's why I am here, more than any other reason: to speak the truth of the Gospel into a needy church and a needy world. This is what all those brothers and sisters who have walked away from the church desperately need to hear: the true gospel. When it comes to our basic understanding of God and our relationship with Him, most of us don't need to hear something new, we just need to believe what we heard the first time!

Jesus + nothing is our salvation and our life.

We need to experience afresh the life of God that is already in us, that never left us and will continue to hold us fast and bring repentance, holiness and godly fruit. The gospel is the power of God unto salvation. The gospel contains God's power to effect radical and lifelong change.

As I have stressed many times over the years, I don't have confidence in my ability to communicate these truths, or in your ability to discern them – but I do have absolute confidence in the Holy Spirit within all believers to energise God's Word and produce the changed lives that we all want. The grace of God will have its own effect - of that, I am sure. That is why grace must be preached over and over and over again.

Many years ago, the Apostle Paul wrote a scathing letter to the Galatian believers after he learned that they had accepted this 'Jesus plus' teaching:

> **Galatians 1:6-7** *"I am astonished that you are so quickly deserting the One who called you by the grace of Christ and are turning to a different gospel – which is really no gospel at all. Evidently some people are throwing you into confusion and are trying to pervert the gospel of Christ."*

Paul can't believe the report he's heard: these brothers and sisters, whose lives were changed through his preaching of the gospel of God's amazing grace, have now thrown their freedom away and accepted something so much less than the full and free life they received through Christ. He's wondering whether he completely wasted his time with them! The Galatians had allowed well-meaning teachers to come amongst them and cut the heart and soul out of the message of Jesus Christ.

The message was simple: *'God loves you and has saved you in Jesus Christ, and He has gifted you an on-going relationship at His expense, with His power – and it's all free to you upon your believing.'* Why does that simple, beautiful message upset anyone? Well, it only upsets those people who have been taken captive by religion. It is a breath of fresh air to everyone else! Jesus and Paul taught that the people who struggle with sin but keep looking to God for forgiveness and relationship, depending on Him to put them right, are closer to the power of the Kingdom of God than those who seem to have it all together. The person filled with the Spirit of God looks to Him for mercy and always finds it. Then God throws in His empowering presence, spiritual gifts and all the blessings of heaven as a bonus!

Whereas the person who seems strong and says: *'Thanks for giving me a start, God. I was lost without You, but I can take it from here. I am going to get my act together, I'm going to memorise the New Testament, and really pay my way. I'll earn my status in the Kingdom of Heaven, so You won't be ashamed of me …'* that person has shifted their focus to their own performance and their heart is full of pride. They have fallen away from grace. The awful thing is that when their life dries up, they will work harder and harder to please God and the more they perform to please God, the more they will suppress the life of Christ within them.

Just like the Galatians, they *'have turned to a different gospel, which is really no gospel at all.'* The true gospel says that God loves us and accepts us just the way we are, through the perfect life of Jesus. His perfect performance against the holy law of God is credited to us and that becomes our experience when we believe, accept and embrace the gospel.

That's the good news. The gospel says that God has already fully and forever taken care of sin. The punishment for the sins of the world fell on Jesus on the cross and killed Him.

The gospel says that God has assured us of abundant life before death and promised eternal life after death because of the resurrection of Jesus. Everything has come to us who believe through Him.

The Gospel is not a set of beliefs and practices – the Gospel is a person: Jesus Christ. Everything He is, everything He has ever done and everything He has ever promised to do is yours and mine and it's all radically free! We just have to believe it and receive it. When we do, all the reality of the gospel will explode within us as we move out in faith and act on what we believe.

Paul is not getting angry because the Galatians turned away from an idea, or a concept, or a set of principles for life. He's upset because they are deserting the One Who called them. When we believe something other than the gospel of God's amazing grace, we don't turn away from a belief system, we turn away from Jesus. No wonder our lives don't work!

The nature of God's grace in Christ is so radical that you get it for free by receiving it, or you don't get it at all. Like any parent, God is looking for our love and a close, intimate relationship.

The only way for that to happen is for Him to cleanse us and set us free … to love Him … or not … with no strings attached. He refuses to deal with us on the basis of our performance.

So, when we turn from Him, and all that He's provided for us in Christ, we pull the plug on the life, substance and power of the Christian faith. So why would anyone turn away from such a relationship and substitute dead religious works? There are many reasons. Grace is risky. Freedom is scary. We might get it wrong. Church leaders who don't understand the basis of grace in our relationship with God may place rules and regulations on us to keep things neat and tidy and controlled in the church.

We've been taught that we have to work to get on in this life – so we're very suspicious of anything we haven't done ourselves. It is difficult for us to believe that our acceptance by God, together with His gifts, power and enabling, does not depend on our performance. Everything of value in this world costs us something, or so we believe.

So, to be offered the most valuable gift imaginable - for free - causes many of us to reject it outright. It sounds too good to be true, and we don't deserve it! I guess that is why it's called the 'good news'! In our fallen, broken world, the gospel is too good to be true, but in God's eternal kingdom it is the Truth and the power of God for the salvation of everyone who believes!

We can also seek affirmation from our brothers and sisters by our performance, so we end up trapped on the 'do-more-try-harder' treadmill and we can't get off. We are happy if we do well and in despair if we fail. It's only in God that we receive true affirmation which is always independent of our personal performance.

God gives us the same affirmation He gave His only Son at His baptism. Before Jesus did any miracles or began 'performing' in any way, His heavenly Father said: *"This is my beloved Son in whom I am well-pleased."* This is not only a possibility for us, it is also our birth right and the single greatest threat to us embracing that birth right fully and experiencing the wonder of our relationship with God in Christ is <u>religion</u>.

Unfortunately, the word religion has been used in a positive or descriptive sense all throughout history to describe the Christian faith. People still refer to that which you and I believe in and live as 'The Christian Religion.' But when you look up the definitions of religion in all the secular dictionaries you will not find one description which contains the word <u>relationship</u>.

That is very interesting and significant because even a quick browse of the Bible will reveal to the most unenlightened, sin-impaired mind that the Christian faith is all about relationship! From Genesis to Revelation, we have the story of God creating us to be in relationship with Himself and with each other.

The whole Bible is about relationships and where they went wrong and what God did to fix that and what we are meant to do (and not do) to participate in His global campaign to re-establish His close, intimate, eternal relationships with His lost children.

I am not talking about man's relationship to God in some abstract philosophical sense here. That is what religion does; that is what philosophy does. I am talking about man's personal relationship with God – one-on-one - an intimate communion. That concept is foreign to religion, and yet that is what the Bible is all about!

That's what the Great Commission is about. That's what the Golden Rule is about. That's what the Ten Commandments are about - and every teaching and instruction from Jesus and Paul and all the other Biblical writers – that's what 'Jesus + nothing' means! It's all about relationship and none of it is about religion. What is religion?

Religion is our feeble attempt to establish and maintain a relationship with God through every means possible other than that which He ordained, provides and empowers.

Some of the most powerful and effective demonic spirits in Satan's army are religious spirits. They are the ones who spend all their time working on Christians like you and me - the same demons who went after the believers we read about in Galatians.

Those believers were totally and powerfully set free in the Spirit and they knew what it was to experience a dynamic, personal, life-changing relationship with the living God in Christ. Yet within just a few short years they had been bewitched by religious spirits and were trying to relate to God through religious works again. We were included in Christ when we heard the truth about our salvation and believed it. At that point the Holy Spirit of God was released in us to make all that real and introduce us to the risen, living, reigning Lord.

In Ephesians 1:3-14, the Apostle Paul states emphatically that everything we could possibly want, or imagine, and even things that we can't imagine, are ours for free. It's all part of the salvation package, and that package is all or nothing. Therefore, we have the following assurance from God in Christ: God chose us and adopted us as a son or daughter and lavished His grace upon us in Christ; our salvation and eternal life with God is a free gift with no strings attached.

Nothing we do or don't do could ever save us, or cause us to lose our salvation; our eternal relationship with God was secured on the cross by Jesus before we were even born – before we could say yes or no, before we could sin or rebel; we have been totally and wonderfully set free by the grace of God to love and serve. There is no other name under heaven by which we can be saved, except the name of Jesus.

The only way into a relationship with the Father is through Jesus, and by accepting our salvation as a free gift - not just once, but every day of our life! To know Him at all is to know Him as a free gift. To participate in His life, ministry and fellowship, we have to understand His grace, because nothing in the kingdom of God is bought, sold or traded. It's all given and received, received and given – FREE!

Do I hear an amen?! It can be hard to learn to receive love from God and others, but it is so important. We also need to learn to give love to God freely in worship, obedience and service; and to love one another in acceptance and kindness. We need that assurance so we can discern the religious traps that would make us slaves to performance again. We need the empowering presence of God in our lives to be able to rest in that assurance, revel in our relationship and be kept free from those influences. The trouble is, they can look so plausible. I'm sure the Galatians would not have chosen to desert the gospel, if they realised that was what they were doing, and nor would we.

But well-meaning Christian brothers and sisters, many of them teachers in the church would say (or imply): *"So you've accepted Jesus ... great start! But now, you need to press on into the higher things of God, by ... having a daily quiet time, reading and memorising the Bible, praying, fasting etc. ... You get in for free ... but you get on at your own expense!"*

Now these disciplines are all great – but they are never a basis for being accepted or not by God. Instead of looking to Jesus alone and being blown away by His love and grace and empowering presence in our life, we are hoodwinked by religion into looking at ourselves instead.

That personal relationship is traded in for our performance and that is so deadly in our walk with God.

The great thing about freedom is that when you know you're free - law, religion, people and even the devil himself can no longer manipulate you. My highest goal for each believer is that you become so secure in God's love and acceptance, nobody can manipulate you or obligate you or make you feel guilty or oppressed in any way … ever again. That is my prayer, and that is God's will.

One of the reasons that the spirit of religion does not want this transforming, liberating grace of God to get out - is because people in the church may do whatever they want to do! Leaders will not be able to crack their legalistic whip and lay a little guilt on people anymore.

God wants you free - He wants you to respond to Him out of love and gratitude and never out of obligation or guilt. Those are the devil's tactics, the world's tactics; that's the flesh - that's religion and you know that God hates religion. If it's not Jesus + nothing … then you've got nothing!

Jesus died to save us from that whole world of manipulation and guilt. That's what Jesus meant here:

> **Luke 4:18** *"The Spirit of the Sovereign Lord is on me, because he has anointed me to preach good news to the poor. He has sent me to proclaim freedom for the captives."*

When you embrace that freedom; when you allow this teaching to get past any barriers in your mind and take root in your heart, you'll find joy like you never experienced in your life; you'll find freedom, spontaneity and a sense of confidence because you will know that it ultimately all depends on God, not you. You will even sleep well at night - because the guilt and sense of not measuring up will be gone. You'll also sleep well at night because you will have worked so hard that day for the Lord for the sheer joy of it! You will pray daily:

"Lord, You've done everything for me ... now what can I do for you?"

It won't take God long to show you what you can do to help fulfill the mission of Christ. It will be hard work and it will be wonderful work - and all done without a shred of guilt, manipulation or a sense of duty.

It will be the natural response of a grateful heart which is overwhelmed by God's love and grace! God will produce this life in you and impregnate you with the ministry of the kingdom of God in Christ. Through the intimacy of prayer, Bible reading, worship, listening and responding to good teaching, obedience, service etc. - this life is then released in you more and more. That is the purpose of those disciplines in our lives – never to gain acceptance or make God pleased with us.

Under the law, prayer, Bible study, worship, service and obedience all become legal requirements. Under grace, in Christ - the exact same activities are transformed in the context of a love relationship and flow from our free love response to a loving God Who has saved us, redeemed us and reconciled us to God forever. The Bible is not a book of answers and rules for life. It is the revelation of God's love and a sharing of His thoughts and His heart.

There will be a lot we will never understand and appreciate about our Lord, but the Holy Spirit has preserved some of His most intimate and revealing thoughts on paper for us and that's how we should approach the Bible and prayer and worship - from the point of a relationship. Loving God will then be our only motivation for any and all of those activities and spiritual disciplines.

Jesus and Jesus alone, is the gospel and He is our salvation. Whenever we add anything as an 'improvement', we have removed ourselves from the power of the gospel and seek once again to save ourselves by our self-righteousness. This is the essence of religious behaviour, which despises God's grace and His free gift of salvation. Religion is an ugly and deadly distortion of what Jesus died to give us.

We experience the freedom we have in Christ when we look to Him alone, not just for our salvation, but for our ongoing walk in the Christian life, depending on Him in all things. Our response is love and gratitude for all He has done for us. He is enough. It's Jesus + nothing! God wants us to live freely in His love and grace, free from sin, free from shame, free from religious expectations and rule-keeping. He wants us to return His love freely, as we learn to know Him more.

So, the choice each and every day for all of us is: relationship or religion? Which will it be for you? Let me remind you of the stark difference between the two.

- *Relationship causes us to be dependent ...*
  Religion drowns us in our own strength.

- *Relationship produces fire and passion in our lives ...*
  Religion produces complacency.

- *Relationship compels us to serve ...*
  Religion drives us to apathy.

- *Relationship draws us towards what's risky ...*
  Religion draws us to something safe.

- *Relationship drives us to our knees ...*
  Religion drives us to our platforms.

- *Relationship births love for the lost ...*
  Religion births love of our rules.

- *Relationship brings change ...*
  Religion forces conformity.

- *Relationship brings forth life and fruit ...*
  Religion brings spiritual death and decay.

Understanding the stark difference between relationship and religion is paramount to understanding the difference between spiritual life and death.

The gospel is not a set of religious doctrines. The gospel is a person: Jesus Christ, and one of the most basic and most important principles for Christian living is that we believe and affirm through our choices, that it's Jesus + nothing!

10. WHAT GOD STARTS – GOD FINISHES

I want to begin the final chapter in this book with the words of the great Dietrich Bonhoeffer, the German pastor whose opposition to Adolph Hitler during World War II finally landed him in jail. Shortly before the end of the war, the Nazis put him to death. At one point he pondered what it means to live in wartime while still believing in all the promises of God. These are his words:

> *"There remains for us only the very narrow way, often extremely difficult to find, of living every day as though it were our last, and yet living in faith and responsibility as though there were to be a great future."*

In writing this chapter, I have pondered again the powerful paradox of his words. On the one hand we are called to live each day knowing it might be our last. That's always good advice, but there are moments in history when it's literally the only way we can live. Prayer can be hard for us. It means giving up the certainty that you have all the answers.

When you pray, you are confessing that there's a realm outside this world, and that God Who dwells in eternity can affect what happens in time and space. Prayer may be our last, best, and only hope in these troubled times. That's part of what Bonhoeffer meant by living each day as if it were our last. But that's not the whole story.

The Christian faith demands that we live in hope because we believe in the promises of God. We cannot become pessimists and give up. To do so is to deny what we say we believe. There is always a reason for hope. So, we come now to the final key principle of Christian living I have for you in this book. Let me recap the previous nine:

1. *He's God and We're Not*
2. *God Doesn't Need Us - But We Desperately Need God*
3. *God's Bidding is God's Enabling*
4. *What We Seek, We Find*
5. *God Responds to Faith*
6. *No Pain, no Gain*
7. *We are Called to Die*
8. *We Live in Two Kingdoms*
9. *The Gospel = Jesus + Nothing!*

The final key principle now brings us right back to God as the beginning and the end of our whole Christian faith: *What God Starts, God Finishes*

This principle gives us hope in tough times and keeps us going when we'd rather quit. It's the truth that inspired believers to be faithful in persecution and gave Moses the strength to exchange the treasures of Egypt for the unseen riches of an invisible God. This truth reminds us that in the end, everything we give up for the Lord will seem like no sacrifice at all. And when life tumbles in around us, and others have given up their faith, we stand firm because we know that what we see is not all there is. The best is yet to come. As I've pondered this truth, these words of the Apostle Pail have been dominating my mind:

> **Romans 8:31** *"What, then, shall we say in response to this? If God is for us, who can be against us?"*

If God is for us, who can be against us? Say that again out loud! When Paul says if God is for us, he's not saying *"Maybe He is and maybe he isn't."* A better translation of the Greek would be: *"Since God is for us"* or *"Because God is for us."* There is no 'if' about it and there is no truth more fundamental than this one: God is for us. God is not against us. God is not neutral toward us. God is <u>for</u> us.

Because of Jesus Christ, once and for all, the question is settled. *God is for us!* All that God is; all that God has; and all that God does; He does on behalf of His people. Even those times when it seems to us that God is acting against us, if we could only look behind the veil, we would understand that God is still for us.

Think of our enemies as the people of God: Can the devil stand against us? No, because he has been defeated. Can the world stand against us? No, because Jesus has overcome the world. Can the flesh destroy us? No, because in Jesus Christ we overcome the flesh. Therefore, let the people of God be bold. Who dares to stand against us if God is for us?

The truth of this principle depends on several important attributes of God. First, God is faithful. That means He does not lie, He does not change in His essential character, and He acts in time and space to ensure that His purposes in eternity are carried out. He perseveres until that which He has ordained comes to fruition.

There are no gaps and no performance failures with our Lord. He is faithful to Himself, to His Word, and to all His creatures. In the end, all things in the universe will be seen to have served God's purposes. No detail will be missing, nothing will be out of place, and there will be no 'accidents.' Even the tragedies of life will fit into God's eternal plan. The fact that we cannot see how this could be true, simply reinforces our first principle: He's God and We're Not! God is faithful whether we see it or not, and God is faithful whether we believe it or not.

Second, God is good. This attribute tells us that God is 'for' us and not 'against' us. He intends to bless us beyond our expectations, and He desires to even bless those who rebel against Him.

Because God is faithful and because God is good, we can be confident that what God starts, God will finish. Sooner or later, His Word will be proven true; His justice will be vindicated; His wisdom will be plainly displayed; and the magnificence of His grace will be proclaimed from one end of the universe to the other; His Name will be glorified; and we will be satisfied. As we work and wait and hope for that day to come, here are three truths you can depend on.

1. All of God's promises will eventually be fulfilled.

The key word here is *eventually*. While reading through the book of Joshua recently, I came across these verses which serve as a summary of God's faithfulness to His people. They come at the end of the section where the Jews have defeated their enemies and have taken possession of the Promised Land. It had been a hard fight that meant some people died in the process. It took blood, sweat and tears to conquer the land and drive the pagan people out. But at last, the work was done, the tribes had received their allotment, and the nation was ready to settle down and live in peace. Against that background, Joshua offers this assessment:

> **Joshua 21:43-45** *"Thus the Lord gave to Israel all the land that he swore to give to their fathers. And they took possession of it, and they settled there. And the Lord gave them rest on every side just as he had sworn to their fathers. Not one of all their enemies had withstood them, for the Lord had given all their enemies into their hands. Not one word of all the good promises that the Lord had made to the house of Israel had failed; all came to pass."*

Note that although the Lord "gave" them the land, they still had to fight for it. The "rest" came only after long years of warfare. They had to go into battle over and over again, and no doubt some soldiers had to die, and blood had to be shed, in order for God's promises to come true.

It's not as if the Jews 'claimed' the promise and then simply moved in with no opposition. They had to fight to win what God had promised them.

So, it is for you and me. We must fight the good fight, stand firm in the armour God has given us, and be good soldiers for the Lord. That means enduring long days and longer nights; facing the fears within and the foes without; being misunderstood by the world and sometimes by our friends; following radically different standards than all the people around us; and claiming dual allegiance to two kingdoms - one on earth and the other in heaven.

Living for Christ means some hard times; bearing the cross; despising the shame; denying ourselves; following Him wherever He leads; judging all things by the values of His Kingdom; putting others above our own interests; yielding our rights; refusing to give in to anger and rage; forgiving when we'd rather get even; loving our enemies; laying down our lives for others; bearing one another's burdens, washing dirty feet; taking on the role of a servant; and sometimes being regarded as fools. Sometimes we will be opposed; sometimes hated; sometimes mocked; sometimes persecuted; and sometimes the followers of Christ will be put to death. It happens.

The point is this, being a Christian does not exempt you from the problems of life. Coming to Christ solves some problems and creates some others. The problems solved include salvation, eternal life, forgiveness, removal of guilt and shame, provision of a brand-new life, new desires, and new power to serve God. And it means a home in heaven and abundant life while you live on earth. So, it's not a bad deal. Not at all. And the problems you gain are small by comparison, but they are problems, nevertheless.

Being a follower of Christ is a wonderful life, it's the best life there is, and it's really the only true life there is. Apart from Christ, there is no life at all. But it doesn't mean that things will be easy or simple or that life will be a bed of roses. Or maybe it will be a bed of roses, but all those roses will have thorns. The good news is that God fully intends to keep His promises to you. What He did for Israel so long ago, He does for His people today. As we trust and obey; as we fight and pray; as we stand up for righteousness and shine the light of Christ into a darkened world, one by one; the promises are kept. And in the end (and not until then) we will look back and say, *"The Lord did it. Not one of His promises failed. All came to pass."*

2. The Lord Will Complete His Work in Us

Psalm 138:8 *"The Lord will fulfill his purpose for me; your steadfast love, O Lord, endures forever."*

The truth here is simple. Because the Lord's love endures forever, His purposes for us will endure forever. If God's love could somehow fail, then perhaps we could doubt His purposes. But since His love reflects His eternal character, we can be assured that God will do whatever it takes to accomplish whatever He wants to accomplish in us.

3. The Entire Work of Salvation is Guaranteed by God

Romans 8:29-30 *"For those God foreknew he also predestined to be conformed to the likeness of his Son, that he might be the firstborn among many brothers. And those he predestined, he also called; those he called, he also justified; those he justified, he also glorified."*

I want you to particularly note five key words in this text: Foreknew, Predestined, Called, Justified and Glorified.

Those five words make up the golden chain of your salvation. It is a golden chain of five links. These five words define the entire work of God on your behalf. No other statement in the Bible so comprehensively explains what God is doing to accomplish your salvation. He begins in eternity past and finishes in eternity future. To say it another way, your salvation begins in heaven, comes to earth, and ends up in heaven. Your salvation begins with the first link - *foreknowledge*. That's the link which starts in heaven.

Then we come to *predestination*. That's the link that brings salvation down to earth. Then we come to *calling*. That's the link where you are hooked onto the chain. *Justification* is the link that ensures your righteous standing before the Lord. *Glorification* is the link that secures your eternal place in heaven.

Notice the tense of the five key words: *Foreknew, Predestined, Called, Justified, Glorified.* They are all in the past tense. But how can *"glorified"* be past tense when our glorification is in the future? How can God speak of our future glorification in the past tense if it hasn't even happened yet?

The answer is this: It is so certain that God speaks of it as past tense even though it is still future to us. In God's perspective, past, present and future are all the same. He is not locked in time and space like we are. So, to God, there really is no past, present or future. It's hard to fathom, but our glorification has already happened. It's so certain that God can speak of it in the past tense. We can be as sure of heaven as if we had already been there 10,000 years. Why? Because it doesn't rest on us. It rests on God. If God has said He's going to do it, He has already done it. What God says He will do, He has done!

Let's wrap this up by looking at some of the ways we can apply this great truth: What God starts, God finishes.

a. We can be certain of our salvation

1 John 5:12-13 tells us that eternal life is only to be found in Jesus Christ and that those who believe in Him may "know" that they have eternal life. In this world of uncertainty, here is something which God says you can know. That's really important.

b. We can be confident of God's purposes for us

This is one of those 'long-range' truths that helps us when we are down and discouraged and wonder if we're all that we were truly meant to be. Philippians 1:6 reminds us that *"he who began a good work in you will carry it on to completion until the day of Christ Jesus."* All that God intends to do in us and through us, He will do. Even when we are faithless, He is faithful (see 2 Timothy 2:13).

c. We can have comfort in the midst of confusing circumstances

So many things in life confuse or perplex us. Things happen, both good and bad, in such seemingly random sequence, that most of the time we can't begin to understand the big picture. But one thing we know is that God is good – all the time. We won't always see how this works out in history, but it is true, nonetheless. "

"For we know," Paul says. Hoe doesn't say, *"we think"* or *"we hope"* or *"we dream,"* but he says, *"we know,"* that *"all things,"* not just *"some things"* or *"most things"* or even *"the things that make sense to us"* he says, *"all things* work *together for good, to those who love God, who are called according to His purpose."* (Romans 8:28).

Because God is good, we will see that goodness manifest somewhere down the road of life, if not now, then later; if not in this life, then in eternity. Everything will be well and God will be glorified.

d. We can remain calm when the world is in turmoil

We live in very troubled times. How do we maintain our sense of balance in a world like this? Psalm 46 points us back to God who is our refuge and strength, a very present help in time of trouble. The word *"help"* means that our God will be for us whatever we need, whenever we need it. He is the supernatural resource when our strength has come to an end. *"Therefore, we will not fear, though the earth give way and the mountains fall into the heart of the sea."* (v. 2). *"Be still and know that I am God."* (v. 10).

Be still. Those who know God can actually remain calm in the midst of turmoil. We know that God is in control. As believers, we do not claim any special insight into politics or military matters. But we know this much: Our God is in control … therefore, we will not fear. We will be still and know the Lord is God.

e. We can have hope when our progress seems slow

All of us, if we are honest, wonder from time to time why we seem to make so little spiritual progress. Sometimes the Christian life seems agonizingly slow: three steps forward, two steps back. Why can't we make 20 steps forward, take a breath, and make 20 more? Why must the Christian life seem so slow in terms of real change?

There are many answers to that question, including the fact that struggle actually makes us grow stronger. We generally do not appreciate victories that come at no cost. What we fight for, we value highly.

1 Thessalonians 5:23-24 tells us that one day we will stand before the Lord and be holy through and through. In that day we will be "blameless" before the Lord, deeply and radically cleansed and profoundly renewed by the grace of God. No part of our being will be untouched. In that day, we will be holy and pure in body, soul and spirit.

Most of us have a long way to go in our earthly life, and we may despair of ever reaching that happy condition. But *the one who calls you is faithful and he will do it*" (v. 24). Our hope rests in the Lord. He called us, He is faithful, and He will do it. In fact, in His eternal kingdom, God has already finished His work in you!

f. We can encourage others who are faltering

The write of Hebrews points us to the crucial ministry of encouragement in light of the Lord's return:

> **Hebrews 10:24-25** *"Think of ways to encourage one another to outbursts of love and good deeds. And let us not neglect our meeting together, as some people do, but encourage and warn each other, especially now that the day of his coming back again is drawing near."*

Eugene Peterson translates the first phrase of verse 24 as, *"Let's see how inventive we can be."* Other translations speak of *"spurring"* other believers on to spiritual growth. How? By a kind word; a phone call; an encouraging e-mail; a friendly smile; and especially by meeting together for fellowship, encouragement, worship and service.

g. We can wait patiently because we know the end of the story

A line in a well-known Gospel song says, *"I've read the end of the Book and we win!"* If you've read Revelation, you know it's true. Jesus wins in the end, and He wins big!

Everyone in Christ wins also! The problem is, right now we're living in an "in-between" time when Christ's victory has been secured but it has not yet fully manifested on the earth. That's where faith comes in. Faith bridges the gap between the now and the not yet of the Kingdom of God.

As you finish this book, it's good to remember what we know and what we don't know. In this life many things remain a mystery to us, especially the troubling issues of personal loss, sudden death, and unexplained suffering. At the end of the day, after all our thoughts and prayers and meditations, and after our deep study of the Scriptures, we simply don't know why some things happen.

Which always takes us right back to the first principle: *He's God and We're Not.* It's amazing how often we come face to face with that reality. But that first principle is basic to all the rest.

If God is God, He must do many things that are far beyond our understanding. But even those things which make no sense to us today, will be seen in the light of eternity to have fulfilled God's eternal purpose. Between now and then, we march onward and upward, moving toward the light that shines brighter and brighter. We march on with faith, hope and love; with deep confidence in the God who made us and who loved us enough to die for us so that we could be with Him. We march on in the sure knowledge that what God starts - God finishes!

www.ingramcontent.com/pod-product-compliance
Lightning Source LLC
Chambersburg PA
CBHW071237020426
42333CB00015B/1519